D0386122

WITHDRAWN
BY
WILLIAMSBURG REGIONAL LIBRARY

Praise for

Gravitational Marketing

"Just spend 10 minutes reading a few pages of this book and you'll be able to crush your competition and make your sales soar!"

Steve Harrison
Co-founder www.FreePublicity.com

"Jimmy Vee and Travis Miller are the Penn & Teller of Marketing. They cut through the BS and reveal the "secret" behind attracting customers. Like all tricks in life, it's a lot easier than everyone thinks it is and Jimmy and Travis make it so anyone can grab more than their fair share immediately."

Doug Huggins
CEO of The Home Ownership Center and
Founder of www.TheMillionaireOriginator.com

"Every business in the world should buy several copies of *Gravitational Marketing* and keep them close by at all times. . . . Why? Because this is a revolutionary book that can turn their businesses around in no time flat! Get this book and get MORE of the best prospective buyers to give you MORE of their money MORE often with MORE efficiency than ever before!"

T. J. Roehleder
President of M.O.R.E. Incorporated

"Want to take your business to the next level? This refreshing book delivers innovative ways to stand out from the crowd and attract the quality of customers you want, need, and deserve. Read it and reap."

Sam Horn
Author of *POP! Stand Out in Any Crowd*

"It's not often that someone puts together *EVERYTHING* you need to know about emotional direct-response marketing, all in one place! And that's not just for 'BIG business' either! This stuff is especially useful for small business owners!"

Scott Tucker
www.MortgageMarketingGenius.com

"Being attractive is hard work unless you can ignore the bad advice given you every day. Marketers by nature don't want to learn anything new, so the few of us who anxiously grab at new thinkers make all the money. That's where Vee and Miller come in, with their Ineffective Ruts Be Damned philosophy. Whoever has the balls to put into practice what it takes to be gravitational will get his money's worth and more. Oh and if you don't care to find out, then ask the person who replaces you to buy this book."

Richard Laermer
Author, *Full Frontal PR and 2011*

"Finally someone does it! Jimmy Vee and Travis Miller reveal how to REALLY attract customers! These guys are outrageously astute marketers. Read this book and you will glean a number of powerful new marketing ideas that you can instantly use in your business. Conversational, insightful, and packed with tons of business building ideas. Pure Genius!"

Kevin Schmidt
International Megapreneur

"This book is contraband! It flies in the face of conventional wisdom and delivers a powerful and fun perspective on what it takes to get customers in today's marketplace. Jimmy Vee and Travis Miller show you how easy it is to attract customers and exactly what you need to do to get them to take notice and seek you out."

Dr. Marvin Lagstein
America's Life Transformation Dentist and
Author of *Brace Yourself for Success*

"This book is full of great tips that are bound to ignite your marketing imagination."

>Kirk Kazanjian
>Bestselling author of *Exceeding Customer Expectations*

"*Gravitational Marketing* is a comprehensive guide . . . that will drive a consistent flow of ideal target prospects to your business. I believe it is a must read for any business owner seeking higher profits."

>Larry Conn
>Founder of www.InstantYellowPageProfits.com

"*Gravitational Marketing* takes lofty ideas to even greater heights."

>Jay Conrad Levinson
>"The Father of Guerrilla Marketing" and
>Author of *Guerrilla Marketing* series of books

"Read this book because YOU CAN'T AFFORD NOT TO. Travis and Jimmy deliver timeless marketing knowledge transcending all conventions that seamlessly transforms into laser-like tactical programs guaranteed to generate more sales in your business and more money in your pocket than you ever thought possible. Real people achieve real huge results with the priceless wisdom contained within the pages of this text. Pick it up, read it, do it, and PROFIT!"

>Adam Dudley
>Direct response marketer and copywriter

"*Gravitational Marketing* cuts through all the hype and misinformation often surrounding good marketing practices and gives you a road map to achieving measurable success. I strongly recommend it."

>Joseph Sugarman
>Chairman, BluBlocker Sunglass Corporation

GRAVITATIONAL MARKETING

The Science of Attracting Customers

JIMMY VEE
TRAVIS MILLER
JOEL BAUER

Assisted by
JENNIFER MILLER

WILLIAMSBURG REGIONAL LIBRARY
7770 CROAKER ROAD
WILLIAMSBURG, VIRGINIA 23188

JUL   2008

WILEY

John Wiley & Sons, Inc.

Copyright © 2008 by Jimmy Vee, Travis Miller, and Joel Bauer. All rights reserved.

Published by John Wiley & Sons, Inc., Hoboken, New Jersey.
Published simultaneously in Canada.

No part of this publication may be reproduced, stored in a retrieval system, or transmitted in any form or by any means, electronic, mechanical, photocopying, recording, scanning, or otherwise, except as permitted under Section 107 or 108 of the 1976 United States Copyright Act, without either the prior written permission of the Publisher, or authorization through payment of the appropriate per-copy fee to the Copyright Clearance Center, Inc., 222 Rosewood Drive, Danvers, MA 01923, (978) 750-8400, fax (978) 646-8600, or on the web at www.copyright.com. Requests to the Publisher for permission should be addressed to the Permissions Department, John Wiley & Sons, Inc., 111 River Street, Hoboken, NJ 07030, (201) 748-6011, fax (201) 748-6008, or online at http://www.wiley.com/go/permissions.

Limit of Liability/Disclaimer of Warranty: While the publisher and author have used their best efforts in preparing this book, they make no representations or warranties with respect to the accuracy or completeness of the contents of this book and specifically disclaim any implied warranties of merchantability or fitness for a particular purpose. No warranty may be created or extended by sales representatives or written sales materials. The advice and strategies contained herein may not be suitable for your situation. You should consult with a professional where appropriate. Neither the publisher nor author shall be liable for any loss of profit or any other commercial damages, including but not limited to special, incidental, consequential, or other damages.

For general information on our other products and services or for technical support, please contact our Customer Care Department within the United States at (800) 762-2974, outside the United States at (317) 572-3993 or fax (317) 572-4002.

Wiley also publishes its books in a variety of electronic formats. Some content that appears in print may not be available in electronic books. For more information about Wiley products, visit our web site at www.wiley.com.

Library of Congress Cataloging-in-Publication Data:

Vee, Jimmy, 1975–
   Gravitational marketing: the science of attracting customers / Jimmy Vee, Travis Miller, Joel Bauer.
      p.   ;   cm
   Includes bibliographical references and index.
   ISBN 978-0-470-22647-6 (cloth)
   1. Marketing—Psychological aspects.   2. Marketing—Social aspects.   3. Customers—Psychology.   4. Information behavior.   I. Miller, Travis, 1977–.   II. Bauer, Joel, 1960–.
III. Title.
   HF5415.V344   2008
   658.8′2—dc22

Printed in the United States of America.

10 9 8 7 6 5 4 3 2 1

For the ladies who make what we do possible, our wives, Christy and Jennifer, and the little ones who inspire us, our beautiful daughters, Autumn Rose and Ella Madeline.

Contents

Foreword

This book may be too dangerous for you. But you won't know for sure until you read the first three and a half pages of Chapter 1 and all of Chapter 6.

Marketing is changing. The in-your-face, bludgeon-you-into-submission, hard-sell style of marketing is dead.

The Internet killed it. Rising media costs killed it. Media fragmentation killed it.

But it was consumers who buried it forever.

Sure you'll see some companies practicing that antiquated form of marketing and they'll soon be dead, too. Victims of their own inaction. Victims of a lack of effective marketing gravity.

The consumers have spoken.

In a recent Yankelovich survey, 33 percent of consumers polled said that they "would be willing to have a slightly lower standard of living to live in a society without marketing and advertising." 33 percent!

Consumers are fed up and most marketing and advertising experts don't know what to do. But Jimmy, Travis, and Joel do.

They've been on the forefront of studying consumer behavior and have been quietly developing a powerful new marketing process that is changing companies everywhere it is implemented. A marketing strategy so powerful it literally compels consumers to do business with you. It causes consumers to put you in the center of their world, of their experience. They don't just want to do business with you, they *have* to do business with you.

The pull they feel is an undeniable attraction as powerful and natural as the force of gravity.

Jimmy Vee, Travis Miller, and Joel Bauer are on the forefront of a cultural and corporate revolution. They are presenting ideas that have been thoroughly tested and proven under the scrutiny and harsh judgment of thousands of different audiences.

This book is different from anything you've read.

There are no hard-sell tactics. Instead, there are emotionally connected relationships created in instants not years.

There are no artificial personas. Rather, there are customer-driven leaders who lead the masses. If you aren't one, the tingle you feel in your spine right now is the dirt being shoveled into your grave.

There are no attempts at winning creative awards. Only an urging to create responsible messaging that changes the way people think... for good.

Everyone thinks Charles Darwin said, "only the fittest survive." He didn't. But those who understand what he did say and who embrace it are the ones who will not only survive but thrive.

Charles Darwin said, "It's not the strongest of the species that will survive, nor the most intelligent, but the ones most responsive to change."

How responsive are you to change? What about your company?

Gravitational Marketing is your guide to controlling the evolving consumer landscape. It is your guide to navigating and responding to change. Your customers are counting on you but one thing is for sure: If it isn't *your* gravity they feel, it will be *your competitor's* and once they are pulled in, you won't get them back.

Don't just read this book. Implement every key idea in it. Put someone in your company in charge of creating and controlling your *Gravitational Potential*. When you do, your customers will love you, your market will embrace you, and you'll be controlling gravity, not being held down by it.

There is a lot to learn in this book from some of the best thinkers on earth.

Implementation is everything and money follows action.
Start reading and start acting.
Gravity can't wait.
Neither can you.

DAVE LAKHANI
Author of *The Power of an Hour* and
Persuasion: The Art of Getting What You Want
Boise, ID
www.boldapproach.com

Preface

Why another book about marketing? Why a full-blown discussion just on attracting customers? Hasn't it all been said before?

Well, not exactly. And frankly, attracting customers is where it all begins. This is unlike any other book about marketing that has ever been written.

Let us give you a little background. Several years ago, we left the comfort and security of our high-paying jobs to strike out on our own and try to make it as entrepreneurs. We started our first company with $200. We bought a phone and the bank charged us a fee to have an account. We were fast on our way to losing money.

We had no customers, no prospects, and no leads. Travis' wedding was six weeks away. Jim's wedding was six months away and there was no way either fiancée wanted to marry a broke loser. We knew we had to do something and do it fast with less than $200.

You may be in a similar position now or remember when you were. It's do-or-die, gun-to-the-head, make-it-or-break-it marketing in its purest form. We either needed to attract customers immediately or fail. There was no in between.

Thankfully for us, we already knew a thing or two about effective marketing and you will too after reading this book. In our careers as marketing executives, we had worked together to create campaigns and systems for our clients that created instant success. In total, we had invested $96 million of our clients' money and with that generated more than $12 billion in sales. It wasn't our money to spend or keep so we didn't get rich. But we did learn an awful lot in the process about how to attract customers and make them buy.

Armed with that knowledge, experience, and just less than $200, we went to work creating our dream and our fortune. Along the way, we encountered many unique opportunities and met a lot of interesting people, like our coauthor Joel Bauer who motivated and inspired us to increase the size of our thinking.

Fast-forward to the present and you'll see that we have made it. We've turned that first $200 into multiple successful companies and millions of dollars in annual revenue that gives us the freedom and flexibility to spend time with our families, live life on our own terms, and leave a legacy while helping other business owners, entrepreneurs, and sales and marketing professionals achieve the success they're after.

That's what this book is about. You will learn how to turn a measly investment in any business or career into a tremendous success by naturally attracting customers. It's the starting point of true success and wealth and a skill that will serve you throughout your life.

This book exposes the bad advice about marketing you've gotten from coworkers, managers, business partners, friends, family members, consultants, media representatives, books, television, and college classes.

You'll discover little known information about how the most savvy and successful marketers in the world are able to capture more than their fair share of the market with far less effort and money than their competitors.

You'll understand the basic steps you must take to create a low-cost, powerful marketing system that naturally attracts a steady stream of qualified buyers who flow into your business day after day every month for years to come. This is a system that allows you to turn the tables on traditional stereotypes. With it, you will decrease buyer resistance, anxiety, and distrust while positioning yourself as an expert resource instead of being just another salesperson or business. It's a smart system that shields you from price wars and enables you to effectively prevail against fierce competitors, even in a crowded marketplace. Finally, you can terminate the endless process of cold calling, door banging, and barbaric old-school sales bull-work that always delivers disappointing results. You can stop waiting for customers to come to you and begin attracting them at will.

You'll uncover a new way of thinking about traditional sales and marketing and learn why the conventional methods and strategies you believe to be true are obsolete and in many cases counterproductive.

After reading this book, you will understand why so many of your marketing dollars and efforts are wasted and how the old-school way of thinking actually adds to the distrust your potential customers have.

Most business owners, entrepreneurs, salespeople, and marketing professionals feel content with getting their fair share of the market. Some are even content with getting less. This information has been created specifically for the unique person who is interested in capturing an unfair portion of his or her market using a systematic, low-cost, powerful marketing process. This content is not for marketing know-it-alls or people who are unable to accept new ideas.

You will learn how to leverage new information to make the sales and marketing process easier, more effective, and less costly to you.

Above all, you will be free. No longer will you be held captive by your business and the struggle for success. When you can attract customers, you can accomplish anything and you can become the center of a universe you create. Your life and business will become ESP—Enjoyable, Simple, and Prosperous. This is *Gravitational Marketing*. This is your future.

Enough promises, let's get to work. The next step is to turn the page and begin.

Be warned. As Thomas Edison said, "Opportunity is missed by most people because it is dressed in overalls and looks like work."

JIMMY VEE
TRAVIS MILLER

Acknowledgments

O ur many and most gracious thanks go out to these fine people:
To our parents who taught us to believe that anything is possible.

To our editor, Matt Holt, who brought this book into the world. And to the rest of the Wiley team, including editorial assistant Jessica Campilango and marketing director Kim Dayman, for your professionalism and hard work.

To the thinkers who have inspired our thoughts and prompted us to make a difference: Jeffrey Gitomer, Malcolm Gladwell, Seth Godin, Dan Kennedy, Dennison Hatch, Michael York; and the departed Dick Benson, John Caples, Robert Collier, Walt Disney, Benjamin Franklin, Gary Halbert, Claude Hopkins, and Maxwell Sackheim. Without all of you this would be a lonely road.

To Tom Spinks and Kimberly Burleson at Millionaire Blueprints for believing in the power of this book early on.

To Joel Bauer, our partner, for making the introductions necessary for this project to become a reality.

And to all the experts who participated and generously shared their knowledge and experience with our readers: Mitch Carson, Larry Conn, Dave Dee, Craig Garber, Steve Harrison, Doug Huggins, Martin Howey, Dave Lakhani, Pete Lillo, Clate Mask, Ken McCarthy, Alice Mishica, Raleigh Pinskey, TJ Roehleder, Ron Romano, David Scott, Timothy Seward, Tony Wedel, and Scott Tucker.

We thank you all and appreciate you very much.

Introduction

In working with hundreds of businesses, we have discovered that to build or rebuild a business, you must start with the owner. And to build or rebuild the owner, you must begin with the owner's mindset and beliefs.

Most people we encounter suffer from the same common thinking. Whether it's about success, business, money making, or marketing, most people hold on to traditional tenets that poison the mind and cause them to fail.

Before the building process can begin, we must fix the foundation. We must eradicate the erroneous beliefs. We must purge the poisonous thoughts from the mind and replace it all with truth. You have to unlearn what you have been taught.

So before we get to the good advice about marketing, business, and attracting customers, let's clear out the bad advice. That way you will start with a clean slate.

Five Famous Fibs and Fables: The Worst Marketing Advice Ever Given

This is a collection of some of the most common misconceptions we have come across. Belief in these lies can reap havoc in your life, but the truth can dramatically change your outlook for profit and opportunity in the weeks and months ahead. So read carefully as we drop the bomb on traditional sales and marketing.

Fib 1: "You've Got to Pay Your Dues."

"You can't expect results overnight in this business and customers aren't easy to come by." Can't you just hear an old boss or someone you know telling you this? You hear this all the time when you're the new kid on the block.

Think about your first job out of college. Maybe it was a sales position and your father was telling you this. You're frustrated, you're not getting leads, and you're having to cold-call. Your dad or your uncle or your older brother, even your wife is telling you, "You've just got to pay your dues."

Many times if you're starting in a new position, there might be a salesperson there who's already the top dog. Maybe he's been there the longest. This is the guy who walks around with his beer belly flopping over his belt, holding a cup of coffee, walking around the office like he's in charge of the place. And he's telling you, "Well, you can't expect results overnight, kid. . . . You've got to learn the ropes. . . . You're going to have to eat lean for a while and take a back seat to the old timers while you work your way up."

Give me a break. The same thing happens if you own your own business. People tell you that you need to wait a few years before things start to take off and before you can really expect to make a profit. But if you stand in line and wait your turn, you're going to be waiting a long time.

You need to cut to the front of the line. Nobody will keep you from doing that but yourself. This whole concept of paying your dues and not expecting results overnight is nonsense. This is bad information that is made up by people as an excuse for their failure. People fear the responsibility that comes along with success.

People like to think that the reason their business isn't doing well is because of the inalienable truths they believe, such as:

- "I've got to pay my dues."
- "I've got to stand in line."
- "Eventually, if I follow in the footsteps of the fairly successful people before me, I'll get my just desserts and I'll be mediocre myself and I'll have an average business or career."

Imagine someone in his first year, first two years, or for that matter even his fifteenth year running a business or a person in a sales career sitting around wondering why things just aren't going his way. He's thinking, "I need to keep my nose to the grindstone. . . . I need to keep paying my dues and learn the ropes and one day this is going to pay off."

If you go to big cities where they have a lot of nightclubs, you'll see the hot clubs have a line around the block to get in. But there are a few people who have a little extra cash and they go right up to the front of the line as they palm a fifty to the bouncer. They get right into the club. There are certain people who know the tricks and can circumvent the system. They're able to leapfrog the entire line and you can do the same thing in your business if you know the insider tricks.

Unfortunately, people have a herd mentality. We know this to be true. We've witnessed it. You may have noticed this yourself. People like to do the things they see other people around them doing. We are taught in school to stand in line and follow the people in front of us—single file.

Business is no different. Everyone's doing the same mediocre things. Everyone's learning the ropes, waiting his or her turn, paying his or her dues. But if you know the trick, you can jump right in at the front of the line and cut off the rest of the pack. So the question is, "What's the trick?"

When you use Gravitational Marketing to attract customers, you can create an automatic acceleration that supercharges your sales efforts. You can enter a new job or marketplace with a new or even old business all with a bang.

You can explode right onto the scene. You don't have to wait in line. That mentality of waiting in line is for people who want mediocre results over a long period of time. We're not talking about that. If that's you, then you can put this book down right now. We want to talk to the people who want rapid success. Even if you've been in business for a long time and you have been following the herd mentality, it's not too late to go from obscurity to celebrity in a matter of months or weeks.

It is true. Using Gravitational Marketing, you will become an instant expert and command respect. You can become the go-to guy or gal. When there's an expert in town, people believe, "She's the one to see. . . . He's the go-to guy." If you need to talk to the expert, you need to talk to this person. The experts are known and that's who you want to be. When the subject of your business comes up, you want to be the one people automatically think, "That's the business to go to."

Most everyone believes that there's some long process you've got to go through to become this expert. But the truth is that today you can declare yourself the expert and tomorrow and the next day you can be operating as that expert.

It requires you to abandon your preconceived notions about success, sales, and marketing. It requires you to take action, hard and immediate action, and be fierce and determined in doing it. It also requires you to abandon your ego and be impervious to criticism because doing the things that we're going to discuss in this book is not typical. They're not conventional. You may even be criticized for doing these things by other people in the herd.

Everyone in the herd, everyone who's close to you, everyone who you think knows about your business, everyone who you have personal relationships with will look at you like you have three heads if you follow these tactics.

You will be a foreigner. You will be someone people just don't get. You're going to be looked at like you're doing something ugly. And it's not until you achieve success (which doesn't take long) that they start to realize that maybe you were on to something. If you're not impervious to that criticism, you're going to falter before you get rich.

How does ego affect your ability to pull this off? Ego encompasses your concern or your feelings about what other people think about you. Since the herd mentality exists and is prevalent in our society, when you act differently from the herd, the herd is going to look at you in an odd fashion. They're going to think ill of you. That's because people have negative feelings about success. They also have negative feelings about people being able to skip the line and get to success quicker then they have.

Let's reference a book, written in 1970 by Richard Bach, *Jonathan Livingston Seagull* (New York: Scribner). If you haven't read it, we recommend it. You could literally read it in an evening. In fact, Travis did when he was in high school. It's about a seagull named Jonathan Livingston, who had a very strong desire to fly and soar very high, very fast, and nose dive while flying very far away from the shore.

The rest of the seagulls just wanted to stay right around the shore. They'd fly no higher or farther than a hundred feet, just lob around, fly very slowly and just be scavengers and pick up scraps of food left behind by people and other animals. Those seagulls represent the herd.

But Jonathan Seagull wanted so much more. When he went for it and when he tried to obtain his goals and fly faster and higher and farther, he was basically an outcast from the rest of the seagull community. But he had to overcome that. He had that choice. Was he going to be successful or was he going to be a member of the community that was by and large mediocre?

When new ideas and techniques are presented to most people, their ego does not allow them to accept the full value and potential of what the ideas hold. Because of their preconceived notions about sales and marketing and what they think they already know or what they already do know, they start blocking out and reducing the effectiveness and power of the new ideas.

Steven Covey discusses this in detail in his book, *The 7 Habits of Highly Effective People* (New York: Simon & Schuster, 1989). In one of the earlier chapters, he tells the story of an experiment he uses when he does presentations. He breaks the people out into two groups and exposes one group for one second to a picture of a beautiful young woman and then he exposes the other group for one second to a picture of an old woman.

Then he gets the groups back together and exposes the entire group to a composite picture of both the old woman and the young woman for one second. Afterward, only with minor discrepancies, the people who were exposed to the first picture of the beautiful young woman see the composite as a beautiful young woman. The people who were exposed to the first photo of the old woman see the composite as an old woman.

Based on what they've experienced in the past, they see that composite picture in a light that isn't what it necessarily is. They see what they want to see because of what they were exposed to previously. That is how ego and past experiences affect what you see in the future and what you see in the present. You need to overcome that. You need to be able to jump ahead, take the advice, take the new ideas, and run with them.

Let's talk specifically about sales and marketing for a minute. Let's say you're a salesperson and you're cold-calling or you're door knocking, burning up pavement or shoe leather, you're out there pressing the flesh. You're doing the sales bull-work. Perhaps you're a business owner, an entrepreneur, running some advertising. Whatever the case, people are going to tell you, "Look, these things don't happen overnight. . . . You can't get results right away. . . . You have to keep at it for a long time until you finally start to experience results."

We're telling you that's bad advice. If you're marketing correctly and wisely using Gravitational Marketing, you will see results immediately.

Fib 2: "If You Want to Be Successful, You've Got to Work Your Tail Off."

You're probably thinking to yourself, "If I'm going to leapfrog the herd and skip paying my dues, what I've got to do is make more cold calls, make more appointments, and work more hours, right?" But no, that's not what we're telling you. In fact, we're telling you that's bad advice.

Have you ever made a cold call or met a person who's a hot prospect you had a great conversation with and then they told you to call back tomorrow? Then when you called back, they didn't take your call or call back? Then you tried again and you didn't get a call back again and again? It happens over and over.

You rang that person's phone off the hook and you feel almost embarrassed when you see him because he's trying to avoid you and it's obvious he's not interested. But you've been taught not to let up, to be relentless in your cold-calling, to be relentless in your sales efforts, and that eventually he'll crack. You think eventually you'll get the deal if you just keep at it or if you're tenacious enough.

What really happens is you get treated like a salesperson or product pusher. People don't take your calls. People avoid you. They don't like you. They talk to their receptionist about you. They joke about you behind your back when you're not there. They say, "Oh if that person comes in again, I'm going to hide in the bathroom and you can get rid of him for me." Is that what you want? Most people don't want to be an unwelcome pest to other people. It's just not a good feeling.

Have you ever hit the street to try to get your foot in the door? It's like you're an encyclopedia or vacuum cleaner salesman or something. You're just dropping in. You're in the neighborhood or you want to learn a little bit about their business. You've heard all of these lame sales lines. "I'm not trying to sell you anything . . . I'm just on a fact-finding mission to see if there's a fit between the two of us . . . to see if there's a fit between our businesses . . . just want to get a little information . . . learn about your business."

That's the stuff the average salesperson does everyday. It's transparent and it turns people off.

If this stuff is working for you right now, go ahead and keep doing it. But if you're the kind of person who hates that stuff and wishes that there was a better alternative, we're telling you right now there is. But again you need to stop accepting advice from most people. Most people just don't know anything. Most people are broke.

You need to forget the things they taught you in college, in business school, in sales training, or in the orientation at your new job. You need to only be focused on the success that you desire for yourself. Remember, many people view success as a crime, especially in sales and marketing. That's why they allow themselves to be victims of bad advice.

Deep down inside they want this nonsense to be true so they don't have to be successful.

The same marketing techniques that allow you to skip the line and leapfrog over your competitors and coworkers can actually allow you to instantly cease cold-calling, cold prospecting, street bull-working, and all of the unfriendly and dreadful things you're doing currently.

You can create an intelligent system that positions you as an expert and causes qualified and interested prospects to come to you and ask you to do business with them. And that stops you from having to do all the ordinary sales grunt-work like dropping all of those cheesy lines, popping in on people, bothering people, and calling them 25 times just so you can get a return call.

If you want to find the solution, stop cold prospecting, be viewed as an expert, and don't aim to be an average salesperson who earns an average wage, this book is for you.

Here's a true story from our own business that illustrates this example perfectly. In the first two months of our existence as entrepreneurs, we relied heavily on the telephone as a marketing tool. We made the calls ourselves. We were selling a product that cost $4,500 (to use for three months) and we had figured that if we sold only one per week, the compounding effects would make us rich within the year. So when we got a warm lead, we would pounce and make sure the lead didn't get away. One time we made a total of 27 calls to the same individual. We always had to leave a voice mail or got the dreaded "I'm busy now, call me tomorrow" blow off. In the end, we realized the guy was just stringing us along so he didn't hurt our feelings. Instead he wasted hours of our time and cost us money in the form of lost opportunity.

Now, years later, by using Gravitational Marketing, this same guy pops up again. This time, he was pulled in and automatically converted to a sale on one of our most expensive products and we never spoke to him on the phone a single time. Everything happened automatically with no resistance.

This fellow doesn't even know that we (people he now perceives as top experts in the field) are the same two pests who harassed him every day for a month practically begging for his business. If you see him around, don't tell him. It will be our little secret. Clearly, our new method is far superior to the original, conventional method.

It was radio star Earl Nightingale who said, "If you have no successful example to follow in whatever endeavor you choose, you may simply look at what everyone else around you is doing and do the opposite, because—The Majority Is Always Wrong."

It's simply because everyone else makes his or her fair share and has average results, lives, and wages. If you don't want to be average, you can't follow what the average person does. You've got to do the exact opposite.

That's where Gravitational Marketing comes in.

Fib 3: "It's All about Getting Your Name Out There."

You're probably thinking, "If I'm going to leapfrog the competition and I'm going to stop cold-calling, the only way to do it is by getting my name out there, right?"

People say, "You want to build top-of-mind awareness. . . . It's all about getting your name out there." You've heard that before, right? Ad agencies love to tell you this one. Media representatives like it too because it's a great excuse for when your advertising doesn't pay off. They want you to think that it's a good way to measure your advertising.

"Top-of-mind awareness" or "getting your name out there" is not a reasonable way to measure your advertising or marketing. You can't deposit "top of mind" in the bank. You can't pay your bills with name recognition. The same goes for dropping off high gloss, fancy material that you've paid tons of money to print. You're not getting you're name out there. You're wasting money.

Here's what happens. You're cold-calling, you're doing some advertising, or you're doing some networking and you're not getting results from any of it. No one's calling from your ad. No one's answering your cold calls and your networking events are fruitless, right?

What you are thinking in your head or what other people are telling you is, "At least you're getting your name out there . . . You're getting that top-of-mind awareness . . . You're getting your face in front of people, so when the time does come for them to buy, they're going to choose you." Supposedly all your efforts will pay off in the end.

That's what building top-of-mind awareness is all about, so that when it comes time to make a purchasing decision, your name flashes in the prospect's head. The reality is that doesn't exist for you, period. For an entrepreneur, business owner, or salesperson, there is no such thing as top-of-mind awareness. There is no such thing as brand equity. What you need is for people to buy now.

Unless you have a bottomless ad budget, you cannot build image, generate top-of-mind awareness, or create brand equity with dollars. Big name cola companies can do it because they've got tens of millions of dollars to invest in their brand. They're willing and able to wait for a return on their investment, which may take years. Are you?

If you've got millions to put out in advertising and marketing and 10 years to wait for a return, then by all means, spend your time and money getting your name out there and building your brand. But if that's not what you have, if you're a business or individual who needs cash flow and money in your pocket to take home to feed your family with, to put your kids through college with, to go on vacations with, and to do the things you want to do with, then the "get your name out there" people are not the folks you want in your corner.

A very popular marketing method is running advertising endlessly. For example, placing an ad in a magazine and putting it in month after month even though you get no calls. The sales representatives love to tell you that you're "getting your name out there" and that it takes a little while to "kick in." That's a reason for you to continue advertising without results. That's the justification.

Another very popular method is purchasing endless promotional items like pens, coffee mugs, and other items that you start handing out at networking events or dropping off at people's offices thinking, "They'll have my pen around and then they'll call me." That's not going to happen.

Another big problem is people spend literally thousands of dollars on printing sales and corporate identity material such as brochures, pamphlets, booklets, and so on. Now, some of that is necessary, but a lot of it is junk. More than 99 percent of all brochures and business cards out there are worthless. If you've got one, the odds are great that it's junk, too, even if you spent a lot of money on it, even if it looks really slick. And you already know this in your heart because you're handing them out by the hundreds and none of them are coming back. No one's buying. You're thinking, "What did I bother doing this for?" Brochures alone don't make sales.

The problem is that most of your material is given to people who aren't interested in what you're giving them. You're giving it to people who haven't asked for it. And of course we all know that if people ask for it, most of the time it's just a form of blowing you off as a salesperson. They may say something like, "Sure just leave some of your information behind." The only time this information is valuable as a marketing tool is if the information in your promotional material is geared toward advancing the sales process and the prospect takes some sort of action to obtain it. They must truly want the material if they're ever going to take a good look at it.

Gravitational Marketing helps you create promotional material that people actually want and gives you a way to use that material to attract people who are qualified to do business with you. So instead of "getting your name out there," you can create a list of people who want what you have to offer and focus your marketing efforts and energy on only them.

Fib 4: "Advertising Is Expensive."

If you've done any advertising or if you've gotten rates from media, you may know that even a small ad in a local publication can run several hundred dollars or more. Other types of large advertising like radio and television can run many thousands of dollars for just a 30- or 60-second commercial.

Many businesspeople think advertising is too expensive for them and is only for big companies. That belief comes from spending money on advertising and getting no results. They figure, "This advertising thing is only for companies who can afford to waste money."

When you spend any time or money marketing your business, even through cold calling, printed material, a web site, driving around, in a magazine, or on the radio and you don't track and measure the results of those efforts, your marketing is always going to be expensive.

But when you can associate every dollar spent with an equal or greater return, it's easy to begin to see advertising as an investment rather than an expense. The reality is advertising is only expensive when it doesn't work.

Here's an example: If you can spend a hundred dollars in advertising and get two hundred dollars back in net profit, wouldn't you find more places to advertise?

We feel like we need to throw a disclaimer in here so that people don't misunderstand. We don't sell advertising. We just help people make smart decisions about advertising. So we're not trying to talk somebody into advertising for our own profit. Instead, we're trying to convince people to advertise for their own profit. We advise this because it truly is the only way to automate the sales process.

You see, there's a calculated and relatively simple way that you can convert ad dollars into a return instead of an expense. There's a way to use marketing and advertising to attract a steady stream of qualified prospects who bang on your door, flood your e-mail box, and fill your voice mail every day.

The secret is to test your advertising on a small scale first and then explode it once you've discovered what exactly does create a return on investment for you.

So many people jump in and spend a lot of money on advertising. Then, if it doesn't work, they are out of money and say, "Advertising doesn't work." Advertising doesn't work more frequently than it does work. That's the truth, even for the smartest advertisers on the planet. But what the smart people know that everyone else doesn't, is that you've got to start very small. You've got to run small tests that won't break your bank if they fail.

Gravitational Marketing is about rejecting all marketing and advertising that is an expense and embracing any marketing and advertising that generates a return on investment. Gravitational Marketing finally gives you a way to make advertising work (and to know when it isn't working so you can shut it off).

Fib 5: "All You Need Is a Good Product, Good Service, and a Low Price."

Henry David Thoreau said, "Build a better mouse trap and the world will beat a path to your door." If you're not familiar with Thoreau, you may be familiar with the character played by Kevin Costner in the movie, *Field of Dreams* (Sony Pictures, 2006). The character's mantra was, "If you build it, they will come."

This is a huge mistake. It happens all the time. Someone starts a business, opens his doors, then waits for the people to show up. But they never come. Next thing you know, he's out of business.

In other cases, people start out in business and spend months or even years working to perfect the product or service they sell. They constantly delay taking action or getting started because they believe they have to make everything as good as it can be.

The first thing you need to do is focus on getting people to show up. Good customer service and a good product alone aren't good enough. People won't come just for a good product or good service. They expect that. They need a good reason to come. If you fail to provide that reason, they'll go somewhere else.

In our neighborhood, there's a brand new sandwich shop that makes Philly cheese steaks better than what you can find in Philadelphia. But the place is empty and will probably be out of business in no time. A great sandwich alone isn't enough to keep this business afloat. They need to deliberately attract customers.

Gravitational Marketing is about attracting people. It's about making people come to you. You can worry about the quality and service after people start showing up. Don't misunderstand, you do need to have good quality and service, but you don't have to spend all your time focusing on making it stellar until after you have people actually coming in to consume it.

If people don't want your product or service, what good is the quality and service? Having a good product and service alone won't make people buy. It will only make people return.

People also like to say, "Well, I just need to come up with a brilliant idea... like the next Pet Rock or something... If I have a brilliant idea, people will just flood to me and I'll be rich, rich, rich."

We believe that the path to riches is littered with the bodies of pioneers who have arrows stuck in their backs. The pioneers don't necessarily get to their destination. The people who succeed find out what the pioneers have done, copy what they did right, and correct their mistakes. The pioneer, the one who came up with the idea first, is unfortunately left lying on the side of the road with an arrow in his back.

Marketing success is not about perfect products, service, or brilliant ideas. Marketing success is about finding people who want what you've got to sell and finding an efficient way to get the message to them. Once you're an ace at that, you can start perfecting your product and service and coming up with brilliant ideas. That's the order. Most people have it reversed. You have to go into the market first worrying about finding people who want to buy and second worrying about what you're going to sell.

Let's talk for a moment about low price. You've heard it before, "If you just lower your price then you'll get more of the business."

But we see low price as a function of the herd mentality. People feel compelled to be in the ballpark. They feel like they need to be similar in price to their competitors to have a chance.

We completely disagree with that thought process. Our experience has proven that low price is reserved for the people who can't market themselves effectively. If you're competing on price, you haven't established enough value in the minds of your prospective customers.

If all things are equal between a product or a service and its competition, then people will buy on price. Your job is to remove yourself from the commodity game and make yourself no longer equal to your competitors. This will help you create a buying preference.

The bottom line is that it's not about how good your product or service is or how low your price is. Your success in business is dependent on how good your marketing is. Price, service, and selection are all secondary to effective marketing. So stop wasting your time trying to come up with the next great idea or to perfect the idea you have and begin attracting people who will buy from you.

You may be thinking, "How do I do this?" Gravitational Marketing establishes you as an expert. It reprograms prospects to your way of thinking and it makes you the obvious choice in their mind. It allows you to create a powerful buying preference in the minds of your prospects and customers. It ultimately reduces their price anxiety. It allows you to create an apple-to-oranges comparison that causes your company to be compared to no other. It eliminates competition from the playing field.

Final Thought

You're probably thinking to yourself, "Guys, all of this sounds great but my business is different." And somebody may have told you that before. Maybe you've presented a good idea to management or to a coworker or to your business partner and they've said, "That's fine, that might have worked somewhere else, but our business is different." The most successful people in business are able to observe actions and strategies that work in one business and apply them to their own business, even across industries.

All businesses are essentially the same. Cold calling always sucks and rarely works. Most people believe the exact same fibs and fables. They all stand in the same line to get their fair share of the business. The tiny percentage of people who are able to make the move to Gravitational Marketing (the Gravitational Marketing mavericks) are able to command higher prices on their terms and get more than their fair share of the market.

The details may be a little different for your business, but the guiding principals and strategies are all the same. It has worked for thousands of others and it can work just as easily for you. Just imagine what your business will be like when leads pour in every week like it was Christmas at the mall, when the phone rings with interested prospects so frequently that it seems like you were giving away free money or when your e-mail box is filled with messages from people who are asking you to do business with them (instead of filled with spam). Imagine what life will be like when you can stop cold-calling, stop wasting money on ineffective advertising, and start doing business only with people who want to do business with you, on your terms. Imagine what it will be like when you can attract customers at will.

If your imagination is unlimited, we can tell you your business and life will become Enjoyable, Simple, and Prosperous.

PART

The Laws of Gravitational Marketing

The Power of Gravity

*The Force That Allows Some People to Get Rich
while Others Get Left Behind . . .*

C lose your eyes, think about this for a moment. Visualize what your life would be like if your business was ESP. Now open your eyes. How did it look?

When we do this same exercise in seminars, people often look confused. So we ask them if they know what ESP is. We get answers like being able to see the future, to predict something is going to happen, sixth sense, and the obvious extrasensory perception. All of these answers are normally correct, but not in our definition of the term.

To us the acronym ESP stands for something completely different, something we have a passion for, something that can change your life. ESP in our minds stands for Enjoyable, Simple, and Prosperous.

Now visualize your life again, this time with the new definition of ESP. What would your life be like if your business was ESP?

What a huge difference changing your perception just a tiny bit makes. Now, when you visualize that, you can really see it can't you? Can you see what a business that is Enjoyable, Simple, and Prosperous could mean for you?

This is a life-changing thought. You work so hard, every day. Wouldn't it be great if what you did all day was Enjoyable, Simple, and Prosperous? It can be and it should be!

That is our goal. To help you create a business that is Enjoyable, Simple, and Prosperous.

Now listen closely because what we are going to say next is the single most important thing you need to know to create a business that is ESP.

We are often asked if there is a magic marketing pill or a beanstalk bean of the marketing world that can produce giant results with just a few resources. Sadly, there is no such thing, but there is one thing that is vitally important that every business owner, entrepreneur, sales and marketing professional must know if they are planning on reaching their goals and creating a business that is Enjoyable, Simple, and Prosperous.

This single concept has meant success for so many people and is something we urge you to learn, embrace, and follow for the rest of your days. We've put this point on paper next and even made it stand off the page so you would be sure to see it even if you aren't paying close attention.

The single most important thing you need to know if you want a business that is ESP:

> You must be the master of your own marketing.

Read that statement again and really think about it. Now, let us tell you why this is such an enormous point for you to store in the forefront of your already crowded mind. If growth is your goal; if making a profit is your goal; if getting customers is your goal; if having a business that is ESP is your goal; then marketing is your only option. You must market or you will get nothing:

- No business.
- No growth.
- No customers.
- No profit.
- No joy.
- No simplicity.
- No prosperity.

All you'll be left with is hard work, frustration, and lackluster performance.

In today's world of commoditization and information overload, it's getting harder and harder for businesses to stand out from the crowd.

It doesn't matter if you own a massage parlor, hardware store, IT consulting firm, entertainment center, or any other business. The fact is we're willing to bet that nearly everything you've learned about marketing and advertising is wrong. Dead wrong.

Nonetheless, businesses and individuals continue to desperately throw their hard-earned funds at advertising and marketing opportunities, or waste time on inefficient sales bull-work, like cold calling, only to wish they had not.

For all intents and purposes, you have little hope to ever properly market your business through traditional means. You can only cross your fingers and hope for the best.

This is exactly why we created Gravitational Marketing.

The advertising galaxy is big—really big. And the big guys think they know how to navigate it. Plus they've got the cash to burn and the human resources to use.

But you, you're different. You're the local hero—the bootstrapping entrepreneur, business owner, marketing director, or sales professional who's worked for every single penny you've earned.

And us? We're the marketing experts on your side. We're the guys who only care about what gets you results, not what wins awards.

Quite frankly, we don't care about the big guys or the advertising gurus. Let them spend their award-winning, unaccountable advertising dollars where they will. We care about you—the business owner, entrepreneur, marketing director, or sales professional.

During our careers, we've had a unique opportunity to witness the advertising challenges these professionals face daily. Specifically, the fact that the marketing process is confusing, often misleading, and to most business professionals unbearably expensive.

Never the ones to back down from a challenge, we set out on a search for the Holy Grail of accountable advertising and marketing. Unfortunately, there wasn't one. So we created it ourselves—a step-by-step system that, amazingly, got results. And with that, Gravitational Marketing was born.

The Big Problem for Most People

The big problem for most business owners, entrepreneurs, salespeople, marketing managers—really anybody who's responsible for bringing business in the door—is how to attract the business. If you've ever been in the business of sales (and let's face it, if you own a business, you're in the business of sales and you better be thinking sales because sales is the lifeblood of the company), you've probably sat there at the desk and thought the same thing, "How do I attract customers?"

Let's talk about some of the commonly used methods that most business owners resort to and dislike with a passion:

- You could open the Yellow Pages and start cold-calling.
- You could go out and knock on doors.
- You could ask your friends and family if they know anyone who would be a prospect.
- You could call a customer list from your old job. But it seems like when you need customers the most, they're the hardest to find and everybody turns their back on you.

When we first started our business, we left our jobs with a client list of people we had spent a long time working with. We weren't going to compete with our old company (we had a pretty serious noncompete agreement), but we were going to sell a product that some of our past clients would be interested in. So we decided to call those people we had relationships with first because we figured that would be the easiest customer to sell.

What we found was that when we called them, even though we had relationships with them from the past, because we had left the old company and now we were working on this new endeavor, we were instantly recategorized as salespeople and product pushers. We quickly realized that we had nothing—not a single decent lead.

That's the category that most business owners, sales and marketing professionals, and entrepreneurs fall in when they're first trying to attract customers. They fall into the category of product pusher, hustler, or salesperson. And let's face it . . .

People don't like to be sold.

Have you ever walked into a business to try and sell what it is you sell and gotten the feeling that they didn't want you to be there? Have you ever made a phone call to a company just to find out if they might be able to use what it is that you have to offer and gotten the feeling on the other end of the line that they really didn't want to talk to you?

Have you ever been at a networking meeting and met someone and had a conversation with them, then when you suggested that you should meet professionally to discuss how your product or service might help them, they suddenly clammed up and did not really want to talk to you? Next thing you know, they're not even returning your calls. This is what the sales prospecting process is like for a lot of people.

It's banging on doors, it's burning up shoe leather, it's making cold calls and being hung up on. And the traditional mindset is if you'd just keep making the calls, you'll eventually hit gold. That is the truth. But it's a hard road to travel.

There Must Be an Easier Way

The good news is this book is going to talk about an easier way.

Have you ever walked through a mall and been approached by a guy with a fantastic lens cleaner for your glasses or a helicopter that zooms out of your hands and flies or a boomerang? Of course. Jim used to do that when he sold puppets in the mall from a kiosk during college. He used to approach people with the puppets and try to get them to come over.

When you walk through a mall and that guy comes over with the puppet or the boomerang or the lens cleaner, you literally steer away. You make a wide berth around him, trying to avoid him at all costs. People would try to avoid us like the plague.

Travis used to work at an electronics store in the mall when he was in college and he would offer free cell phones to people. He would stand out in the mall and would basically call out or barker to people as they would walk by and offer them a free cell phone. They would literally walk to the other side of the aisle.

Barker is an interesting word we chose to use. We believe that most people, because of the traditional way they are taught to sell, are barkers. A snake oil salesperson is synonymous with barker. People are adverse to barkers. They know their tricks. They have a negative connotation with the barker and the snake oil salesperson. They try to avoid those people at all costs. But when you try and sell your product or service, you are basically that person. It's sad.

The legitimate business owner and the legitimate marketing director or salesperson who's offering a legitimate service to people, a service people could really use or a legitimate product that could really help them, do not get a fair shake because people avoid anyone who's trying to sell something at all costs. This creates a problem. This singular problem is what causes most small businesses to fail or big businesses to fall stagnant. It's what causes many businesses to have to spend an enormous sum of money on advertising or put an enormous number of salespeople on the ground to attract a small number of interested potential clients.

The Best Marketing Wins

The difference between a company that is successful and a company that is struggling is usually defined by one thing: The company that is successful has lots of customers and the company that is struggling doesn't. If we need lots of customers to make it, wouldn't it be better to have the customers come to you instead of you having to go out and chase them down?

If the person with the most customers wins, then by the same definition, it's the company that understands how to attract the most customers that's ultimately the most powerful.

Here's the solution. Here's what you need to learn how to do. You need to learn how to transition from having to go out and chase down customers to understanding how to attract or gravitate customers to your business. That's exactly why we created Gravitational Marketing.

When we had jobs, we devised a method to cause people to flock to our clients' businesses. It was very effective. But the problem was it was very expensive.

It delivered an excellent return on investment but what we realized was that many businesses just could not, under any circumstance, play that game because they didn't have the necessary cash to do it. And the necessary cash usually meant a minimum of $30,000 per month in advertising and as much as $100,000 or $200,000 per month in advertising.

So we asked, "How can we duplicate or replicate those results causing people to come to us—to come to our clients—but without spending all of that money?"

We locked ourselves in our office, which happened to be a small room in one of our houses. Every day for months and months we would hole away in that office and try and solve this problem.

We tried different ideas and we tested different techniques and we presented different theories. And then one day it all came to us at once.

The Eureka Moment

This simple, little idea would truly make people quickly, easily, and naturally come to you and identify themselves, almost waving their hands saying, "I want what you have to sell." Then you could put all of your focus, energy, budget, and time marketing directly to those people who have already told you that they want what you have to offer, that they want the benefit that you offer, and they've given you permission to tell them about it.

That sale has almost no friction, a higher closing ratio, and typically is more enjoyable to make. It also provides you with a customer who has a longer relationship span, a higher degree of respect for you and your company (which is very important), and a greater level of profitability to your company (which is even more important).

This process, which we called Gravitational Marketing, causes people, potential customers, to raise their hands and say, "Market to me because this is something I'm interested in." That is a powerful thing.

 From the Trenches

A great friend of ours recently forwarded several ad-related articles from a few big-name business magazines including a list of the best ad-related blogs. As I skimmed the articles and the blog postings, a dark feeling crept into my heart: This information is not for those of us down here on Earth.

There was no discussion about the most important aspect of marketing: getting new customers. Instead, the space was filled with discussions of image and art and how to create and maintain a brand for your company.

It seems that these glitzy ad folks have created this world, high above the rest of us, in the clouds, where getting new customers doesn't matter. Looks are more important than leads.

This may be fine for Coke, McDonald's, Nike, Sony, Tommy, and the like, but it doesn't do a bit of good for those of us down here on the ranch.

My big problem with all of these major ad blogs and the major ad and business magazines is that they reside in the land of the brand. That's not where we are. That's not where our clients are.

None of these blogs discuss real concepts for getting prospects to call you or bang on your door. I read the business magazines every month and have decided they are deadly to an entrepreneur starting a small business. I'm not saying their ideas aren't good, or the concepts aren't sound, or the information is bad, or the writers are dumb. But I am saying it's the wrong information for the small guy. And most of us are the small guys.

The big companies are controlled by a small number of executives and Madison Avenue firms. It's the rest of us, the majority of us, who represent the sea of small businesses trying to pull it off in the Now Economy.

The more I learn and the more I see, the greater the divide seems to become between what's real and what's scented, glossy magazine fantasy. It's like a woman reading a fashion or beauty magazine and believing her life and looks should be like those discussed in the articles or shown in the pictures. It's really no different.

Big business magazines paint pictures and tell stories of eclectic companies with execs who wear sneakers and Mohawks and drive electric cars—and oh, by the way, that's the extent of their marketing. It may be true. About as true as Brittany Spears'

(continued)

first wedding was—but that doesn't mean it exists down here at ground level where the rest of us are working to pull a buck or a million.

So why don't these scented, glossy magazines portray the bootstrapper who started with a 1,000 piece direct-mail campaign and a small ad in a trade publication and turned it into a million dollar business?

Because it's not glamorous, it's not sexy, and that girl doesn't have a Mohawk.

Well, neither do you or I.

The take away here is to understand that these magazines' jobs are to sell magazines. Sensational stories sell magazines. Great.

But small business owners and entrepreneurs everywhere must be very careful and aware of this truth and be cautious not to let their brains be filled with self-doubt, envy, or disappointment that their businesses and their marketing aren't like those in the magazines and blogs. They're not supposed to be.

 Expert Resource

Millionaire Blueprints is a magazine we recommend that all business owners read because it gives real-life examples of how everyday entrepreneurs have gone from broke and struggling to millionaire status. The magazine interviews these bootstrapping entrepreneurs and gets them to reveal their secrets so you can use them to grow your business and achieve similar results.

We personally read this magazine and love it. It's the only magazine we race to the mailbox for. You can learn more about *Millionaire Blueprints* magazine by going to the Gravitational Marketing resource site at www.GravityBook.com/blueprints.

Anatomy of Gravitational Marketing

*Attracting Customers by Harnessing the Power
of a Natural Force . . .*

G ravity is abundant, and best of all it is free. Gravity is a natural force that exists whether we like it or not. The ability to leverage gravity and bend its force in your favor is a powerful opportunity that exists for anyone who needs to attract new customers.

Science of Attraction

Gravitational Marketing is based on the principle that all bodies exhibit an inherent force called gravity that naturally attracts other bodies. Following that analogy, every business has a natural tendency, however large or small, to attract customers. Larger companies traditionally have a stronger gravitational force. Smaller companies traditionally have a weaker gravitational force. The potential of the force is affected by several factors such as a company's location, signage, current marketing and advertising efforts, and word-of-mouth advertising. As the force grows, it builds momentum and allows you to attract exactly the right group of prospects and customers without wasting tons of money.

Our method levels the playing field and gives businesses that have limited marketing and sales resources an opportunity to increase their gravitational potential without drastically increasing their marketing costs or the size of their company. Continuing the analogy, Gravitational Marketing helps companies defy the laws of gravity by attracting more than their fair share of the business.

Gravitational Marketing has its roots in direct marketing, good old-fashioned relationship building, and a concept we call "sensational" which is a surefire method for standing out and getting noticed. Gravitational Marketing is essentially a combination of direct response marketing techniques, differentiation tactics, and solid communication and management strategies. It allows business owners and individuals to systematically attract leads and convert prospects and even strangers into fans and repeat customers, all without wasting time, energy, or money.

Gravitational Marketing is the process of motivating prospects to ask for your marketing messages, forging emotional relationships with prospects, getting your newly formed friends to buy, motivating existing customers to return, and ultimately causing all of your customers to tell others, thereby harnessing the power of word-of-mouth advertising, which we all know is the best and cheapest form of marketing.

Once you fully understand and learn how to use Gravitational Marketing, you will spend less on advertising, have better relationships with your potential and existing customers, and have a virtual salesforce working day and night for you for free.

Three Rings of Gravitational Marketing

Gravitational Marketing is comprised of three elemental rings: market, message, and media (see Figure 2.1). Each ring is as important as the others and if any one ring is broken or incomplete, the power of your gravitational potential will be reduced. The rings are not

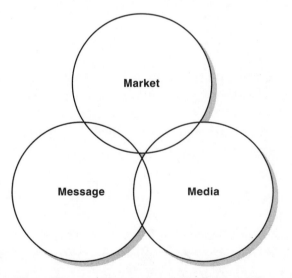

FIGURE 2.1 **Three Rings of Gravitational Marketing.** These rings show the three main components of a gravitational marketing campaign. The rings, although independent, work together to create a productive and profitable campaign. Without synergy between rings, you have a disjointed campaign that will not resonate with prospects, or worse, may never reach them.

separate entities each with their own beginning and end. Instead they are interconnected, linking rings; each one affecting the others.

Market

It doesn't matter much what you say or where you say it if you don't know who you are talking to. Marketing that lacks a target is marketing that lacks results. Our world is made up of many different types of people all with unique desires, pains, experiences, emotions, situations, hopes, dreams, and fears. There's no way to know exactly what each person is thinking or feeling, but similar people think and feel in similar ways.

By focusing on a specific group of people or groups of people—a specific market, you can customize your marketing to be a perfect fit for people in the group.

> A clearly defined market gives you clarity, purpose, and direction.

Message

Once you know who you're talking to, your ability to create a message that resonates with those people is significantly greater. An effective message is at the core of effective marketing. Your message is what communicates what you offer, the problems you solve, the hopes you fulfill, and the reasons people should care about you or your product or service.

Media

With the clarity of a target market and the potency of an effective message, you're ready to choose the media through which you will deliver your message to the market.

The media are the vehicles you use to deliver your message to the marketplace: Newspapers, magazines, television, radio, direct mail, the telephone, networking, and the Internet. Which media you use will be dependent on who is in your market and what your message contains.

How Gravitational Marketing Works

The process of Gravitational Marketing is broken down into four primary components: Gravitate, Captivate, Invigorate, and Motivate.

Step 1: Gravitate

The process begins by either choosing who it is that your existing product or service would be right for or by finding the who first and then determining what they want. We call this targeting.

Next you find out what problems they're having, what difficulties and challenges they face, or what they really want but have to live without. And you offer the solution to that problem, whatever it is. For instance:

- If you are a financial planner, the people that you're going to help want security, they want to retire wealthy, and they want to retire early. They don't know how to accomplish these things. That's their problem.
- If you're a real estate agent, the clients you will help want to sell their homes as quickly as possible for as much as possible or own as much home as possible for the lowest payment possible. That's what they want from you. Nothing else.
- If you're a car dealer, the people you want to help are in need of a car but they are afraid of getting taken advantage of. They want to make sure that they get the best deal possible.
- If you're a marketing consultant, the people that you are going to help want to get new business and they need to know how they can do that.

The list goes on and on.

So you offer a very simple initial solution that only requires a small step, a small type of action with little commitment and zero risk.

It's almost like a piece of bait. It's like saying, "I've got the answer to your problem—come to me and I'll explain."

At first glance, this may seem like regular advertising, but indeed, it is very different.

Step 2: Captivate

The Captivate phase happens once you've gotten your prospects' attention. They've asked for more information about the solution that you're offering and you have a chance to present yourself to them. But you have to present yourself in a way that is unforgettable. You can't just be another "me too" service or a commodity product. You've got to be sensational. You've got to be memorable. You've got to be unique. You must captivate your audience in order to hold their attention, arouse child-like curiosity in them, and cause them to be intrigued and to want to know more.

Step 3: Invigorate

You Invigorate your prospects by helping them understand how bad the problem actually is that they're facing now and how wonderful the solution really could be. You must get them to visualize themselves living the dream.

You need to involve their emotions in the process and help them understand the depth of their problem but also the true availability of the solution and the wonderful things that will come with the solution.

Step 4: Motivate

Finally, you have to Motivate your prospects to take the action you want them to take. That means you have to know ahead of time what that action should be. You can't just arrive at the Motivate phase and not know how to proceed and let the prospect direct the transaction.

With a clear vision of the desired action, you can overwhelm the prospect with benefits, bonuses, offers, and value that make doing business with you irresistible.

Each step of this process is critical. If you fail to attract prospects (Gravitate) in the first place, nothing will happen. But once you've attracted the prospects, if you don't capture their attention (Captivate), you will become invisible and the sale will be lost. Even if you have captured their attention, if you don't involve their emotions and get them excited (Invigorate) about the possibility and potential of working together, the game is over. Finally, if everything has come together but you don't cause the prospects to take the final action (Motivate), if you don't ask them to spend money, all of your efforts will have been wasted.

A Unique Focus

This book is an in-depth look at the Gravitate phase that causes qualified prospects to come to you. You'll learn how to get prospects to identify themselves as people who need and want what it is you offer.

We'll teach you how to make prospects come to you with little effort, give you permission to market to them, and let you begin the sales process. Our focus here is on lead attraction for one reason and one reason only. It's the area where most people need the biggest amount of help. This is the part of the process where most people struggle and fall short. And you can't Captivate, Invigorate, or Motivate until you've caused prospects to Gravitate to you in the first place.

Most people have a decent enough sales process in place so that once a lead is generated they can convert that lead. Then they usually have a system in place to deploy the product or service. They sometimes even have a system to follow up with customers on a regular basis and get them to return and do business multiple times. But sales can't even start until the lead generation process is in place. And lead generation is broken or doesn't exist in most businesses.

What we found most business owners and companies lack is a strong and automatic process for taking people who are strangers and converting them into prospects. This book is all about that simple process.

How to Be Worthy of Attraction

Why People Will Be Attracted to You above All Others . . .

Since we're talking about the process of attracting customers, it's only fitting to discuss a method of being worthy of attraction.

Let's face it. No online dating site will be any help to an ugly fellow with an awful personality and bad breath. He has no hope. Likewise, if you fail to present your company in a favorable way, even the best marketing will be useless.

It makes good sense to stack the odds in your favor and give yourself an unfair advantage by turning you and your company into something irresistible and unforgettable. That's what we call sensational. Being sensational is something that any business, small or large, can do with just a little attention to detail and a small amount of creativity. Sensational companies have a greater Gravitational Potential than unsensational companies. The best news is that being sensational doesn't have to cost a lot of money, if any at all. It's a fantastic way to give your business an immediate boost just by looking at things a little differently.

We've identified seven B's in being sensational.

Be Interested

If you're going to be sensational, you have to be sensational to other people personally. They have to like you. You have to be interesting, fun, funny, and conversational. You have to have similar interests and get to know them. You have to understand them and be easy to talk to. You have to be comfortable and friendly.

Well how can anyone be all those things? We know, "You don't have that type of personality," right? *Wrong*. Everyone can have this type of personality if they want to.

It's very simple to be these things to other people. But most people can't do it, won't do it, or don't know how to do it, but it's simple. Here is the secret to being the kind of person that everyone likes:

Shut up! Be interested in other people for a change.

Shut your mouth and let the other person talk. Ask the other person about himself or herself and be quiet. Acknowledge that you are listening, interested, and enjoying what they are saying by nodding, making gestures, and asking additional questions. Leave long pauses so that they can fill in the gaps with more information about themselves. Always talk in terms of them. If they ask you a question, answer as thoroughly and quickly as you can, and then relate the question back to them.

In a conversation, if you listen 90 percent of the time and talk 10 percent of the time, people will think you are everything we discussed earlier. They will feel a strong connection with you, a bond, and a friendship. Guess what? People do business with people they know and like.

The two biggest snags with this are (1) people don't know how to shut up and listen, and (2) you have to be genuinely interested in other people. You have to genuinely like people. If you are just standing there going through the motions, people will not like you, and they will know immediately that you are not genuine.

So be genuine, be interested, and be sensational.

Be Unique

If you're going to be sensational, you have to be worth looking at, worth taking notice of. I know you are asking yourself, "But how do I do that?" You need to be interesting. You need to be unique.

There is no substitute for uniqueness. By going against the grain, doing the opposite of the people around you, you will automatically stand out. Standing out is always better than blending in. Most people and businesses are earth tones in a world of drab colors, camouflaged, purposefully unnoticed. That's not good when your goal is to attract customers.

Because you are generally a direct representation of your company, you need to try to be unique yourself. But also, your company and product or service needs to stand out. Those who stand head and shoulders above the rest will generally profit.

When you walk into a crowded room, you notice two things subconsciously about the people in it: the tallest and the shortest. Why? Because they are outside of the standard deviation, they are at the ends of the bell curve.

As humans, we have been programmed to notice things that seem different and out of the ordinary. We are almost naturally attracted to them. No one immediately notices the people in the middle. They all seem to blend together.

Why are some people considered dynamic and others not? The same reason some companies are dynamic and others are not, the same reason some products are dynamic—because they stand out. Something about them makes them jump out at you, makes you take extra notice, and creates an emotional stimulus within you. They are unique; they are interesting.

Don't be shy. Shy and unique are two things that do not go together. You must be bold.

In our marketing careers, we have worked with many companies in the automotive industry. An auto manufacturing expert once told us something that we haven't ever been able to forget. It stuck with us, and we'd like to share it with you because it embodies the heart and soul of being unique.

He told us that smart auto manufacturers design and build cars based on what he called the *Rule of Thirds*. Have you ever noticed a new vehicle on the road and said, "That is awful, ugly as sin, who would ever buy that thing?" If you have, that car likely was designed and manufactured under the Rule of Thirds.

Have you ever seen a car on the road that stopped you dead in your tracks, gave you whiplash trying to watch it go by because it was so incredibly good looking? That car was also manufactured under the same principle.

The rule says that every car should cause one-third of the people to absolutely hate it and one-third to absolutely love it. The remaining one-third just don't pay any attention. If the manufacturers built a car that catered to the preferences of the majority, nobody would be particularly passionate about it. It would blend in and just go unnoticed. More than likely, that would leave price as the only differentiation factor for that vehicle.

When you are truly unique and interesting, you naturally and automatically attract a portion of the market that you wouldn't attract otherwise. At the same time, you naturally and automatically deter a portion of the market that doesn't like something about you. The rest of the market isn't paying any attention.

We'd gladly take the opportunity to have one-third of the people love us while one-third of the people dislike us over dealing with 100 percent who are indifferent or who never even notice us.

We like to think of uniqueness as *antichance*. It's the opposite of hoping that people will take notice of you. Instead it gives them an undeniable reason to pay attention. Whether they like you or not, you will get their attention.

Be unique, be interesting, and for goodness' sake, be sensational.

Be Fun

What does fun have to do with business? Fun is fun and business is business, right? Not really. Business should be fun for you and fun for your customers and your employees, too.

Lighten up. There is no business that is so important that you can't be human. Not medical . . . ever hear of laughter being the best medicine? Not law . . . that field needs a bit of fun to liven things up anyway, plus there are more attorney jokes than just about any other kind. Not the airline industry . . . Southwest Airlines has changed the game by having a bit of fun.

People respond to fun, humor, and camaraderie. People want to be associated with and hang out with people who are fun. Nobody wants to be stuck in the corner with the boring guy. So don't be the boring guy.

To be sensational, you can't take yourself too seriously. Life can be serious, business can be serious, and relationships can be serious. That's enough serious for everyone.

People have to be loose, fun, flexible, and dynamic. It's a balance.

An interesting quote by Jean Cocteau makes the point: "Angels fly because they take themselves lightly."

Who would you rather hire to do a job? Someone who is qualified but is always in a bad mood, stressed, and seems miserable or someone who is qualified, fun, easygoing, and relaxed?

So now you're fun. You need to incorporate the fun into your business. Make the customer experience fun. When people experience your product or service, make them feel the fun. Work it into the core of the company. Make your employees have fun.

It is not enough to be fun yourself. You must have the fun factor integrated into the core of the company. It must be a fun place to call, a fun place to shop, a fun place to drive by, and a fun place to tell people about! You can't make all of this happen by yourself. You can't be the Grand Pooh-Bah (the *Mikado*) of fun without the help of your team.

Your employees are your first line of defense and offense. They are usually the first to greet your customers. If they don't believe, see, and buy into the fun concept, they will not deliver the message where it matters most—to your customers.

Be fun, be sensational.

From the Trenches

I'm sorry to admit it, but my wife and I frequent a particular fast-food taco joint. I've noticed in the past few months since they opened that their operation spins like a top. The place is usually spotless, the environment is comfortable (for a fast-food joint), the service is lightning fast, and the employees are generally friendly and somewhat conversational.

Interestingly, several employees have made negative comments to me about their manager (who is basically a fixture in the place). You must understand I have a tendency to ask probing questions whenever I'm at a business—because I'm interested. But I find it interesting that more than one worker has a problem with the same manager and is willing to spill their guts about it.

(continued)

Today I stopped in and guess what? The manager wasn't there. Guess what else? The place was a wreck. It took over 10 minutes to get our food, there were no straws, the sauces were piled up on the counter in cardboard boxes, ice had overflowed the drink fountain and was spilling onto the floor, and the restaurant wasn't even busy. Instead, these people were just lost in space—it never even occurred to them to come out into the restaurant and check on things.

It sounds like an all-too-common tale. And maybe it is. But I have several points to make:

- When the boss is away, the workers will play. So be prepared.
- The success and failure of your operation isn't necessarily tied to whether or not the folks in the office like you. This manager wasn't liked, but she ran a tight ship (at least when she was there).
- All of the best marketing efforts break down at the point of sale. Marketing can easily become the biggest investment you make in your business. It can quickly trump your rent and your payroll. And for good reason. Done correctly it can earn a much larger return on investment than anything else you do. But watch out! Even if you don't own a taco stand and even if you don't have employees, you can be a victim of the same trick. Vendors, colleagues, competitors, and even you can be your worst enemies at the point of sale.

Think about your own business and the process the customers you've paid to get must go through to do business with you. Is it worth paying for? Would it be worth returning? Would it be worth talking about? More important, when your back is turned, is it the same as it is when you're looking?

Michael York (www.michaelyork.com) suggested to us recently that real change within an organization comes from personal development. At first that may seem obvious, but it's worth another look.

Clearly, the workers at the taco place were submissive to this mean manager when she was there, but rebellious when she was gone. And why not? What kind of personal development is going on there? My guess is not much.

Your business should be different, and if the people within it, including yourself, are not doing something to develop themselves personally, then you are all paying the price.

What separates leaders from managers? I submit to you it is the ability to spark a small flame within the belly of someone else. I don't believe the taco boss is sparking many flames in bellies (although I feel a little something hot in my belly right now).

What flames are you sparking? Don't worry about finding the perfect flame, either. Just pick something to be passionate about and start spreading it. Perhaps integrating fun into the team experience could cure the negative feelings employees have about the boss at the taco stand and cause the boss' influence to extend beyond her physical presence.

Passion sells! It sells everything from your customers to your employees. Your passion for certain ideals and goals will rub off on those around you and cause them to buy in.

Be Visible

Believe it or not, you can become more sensational just by being more visible. Visibility simply means being seen. But, to be truly sensational, you must go to the extremes.

Be seen everywhere. Be seen constantly. Be seen by everyone. Consistent visibility leads to heightened credibility. So how do you drastically increase visibility?

Volunteer

Get involved with your favorite nonprofit organization. Don't just show up. Take charge. Get on the board or lead a team. Chair an entire event.

Donate your expert services to the organization in exchange for a little recognition.

Many nonprofit fund-raising events involve months of planning and draw crowds of thousands. You can spend those months of planning bonding with other volunteers in your town and benefit from the recognition you'll receive on the big day. Not to mention that you'll feel great doing it.

Network

Get involved in chambers of commerce, leads groups, social clubs, business journal events, trade meetings, and so on. Show up and listen.

Create a game of trying to identify people's problems then connect those people with someone that you know can help them. Take it a step further—get on the board, chair a committee, plan an event. Do anything you can to be more visible than your competition.

Publicity

Give a free seminar, host an event, write a book, and then tell the local press about it. There are even online press release bulletin boards that can make your company name or your name show up in the search engines attached to the news stories.

The idea here is to get your name printed in as many papers and on as many web sites as possible. You'll definitely get noticed when you do.

Events

Throw an after-hours get-together at your office. Have a holiday party and invite the members of all of the organizations you're affiliated with. Get a booth at the local festival. When people get together, do whatever you can do to be at the epicenter.

Advertising

Advertising, of course, is visibility that you pay for—print ads, direct mail, billboards, radio, and television, even the Internet—but it has some very big benefits. You can specify what you say, whom you say it to, when you say it, and how often you say it.

There are a few large caveats:

- Be consistent or you will see poor results.
- Don't spend money on advertising that doesn't work (that means you have to test and measure your efforts).
- Get professional help writing, designing, and producing your ads.

If you use a combination of these ideas to increase your visibility, you'll soon realize how few of your competitors are taking advantage of the same opportunities. It takes work, but if it didn't, everyone would be sensational.

Be seen, be visible, and be sensational.

Be Credible

As we said earlier, consistent visibility leads to credibility. Another very quick path to increasing credibility lies in positioning yourself as an expert.

Being an expert is part of being sensational and can increase profits significantly while bulletproofing your net profit against your competitors at the same time.

In the next chapter, we'll talk more about how you can rapidly position yourself as an expert.

In addition to positioning yourself as an expert, capturing and featuring proof (like testimonials from enthusiastic clients), writing articles for trade magazines, local newspapers, and special interest publications, or having news stories written about you can also be a fast track to credibility.

> People are far more likely to believe something someone else says about you than something you say about yourself.

Leveraging credibility serves to decrease buyer resistance and distrust and helps you actively attract new prospects more rapidly with a smaller investment. Credibility makes marketing easier. Sadly, most businesses underutilize credibility and overlook this tremendous opportunity.

How many businesses have you encountered that haven't mentioned a single testimonial or used expert information to make their case and enhance their credibility? Most businesses don't do it—they just expect the customer to do the research and the legwork, which most people won't do. But it's an extremely low-cost and high-yield effort that can explode with results.

Be credible, be an expert, (let's say it out loud and together) be sensational.

Be Spreadable

Yes, we made up the word. The coup de grâce of being sensational is this: you are yearning to be talked about. You know that word of mouth is the most powerful form of advertising. Spreadability is the mechanical complex that allows it to happen most rapidly and predictably.

Take a moment and visit www.subservientchicken.com.

Believe it. It really is a man wearing a chicken suit, and yes, he takes orders. Did you "tell a friend?" If you did, you're not alone. That web site received 20 million hits within the first week.

Aside from being ridiculous, it is an advertisement for Burger King's chicken sandwich. Now you can finally have chicken *your way*.

This is a crude, but sensational example of spreadability. What's going on here is called viral marketing. You've participated in viral marketing whenever you've sent a joke to a friend, told a coworker about a new restaurant, or referred a neighbor to your plumber.

It's nothing new. But new technology allows us to control it more than ever. In fact, there's an entire science related to the diffusion of ideas through a population and it's more complex than it appears on the surface.

Here are a few ways to get your name, your product, or your sensational idea to spread. That's the goal, isn't it?

Viral Marketing

Create something that is very interesting. It might be information, it might be entertainment or, as in the case of the chicken, it might just be weird. Then, share that something with people who are well connected. You know who they are … the folks who seem to know everybody.

Put your *virus* in their hands and they'll bounce it around like a hot potato as long as it's very interesting. Your brochure doesn't count.

Pass-It-On Program

Give a gift certificate (not a coupon) to every one of your customers. Put their best friend's name on it. What are they going to do? Gift certificates are like cash, so they're not going to throw it away.

What about the best friend? Well, it would be rude to throw away a gift from your best friend. Chances are those friends will soon be knocking at your door.

Bring-a-Friend Program

Bring a friend who has never been to our restaurant and we'll buy you both a glass of wine. Pretty simple idea, but very under appreciated.

The most important part of any effort to increase spreadability is to be sensational. If your message, product, service, or idea is ordinary, it will flop face first into trash bins and deleted items folders around the world. That wouldn't be sensational, that would be a shame.

Sensational and the Apple

Being sensational plays an important role in the processes of Gravitating, Captivating, Invigorating, and Motivating a prospect. Now that you understand the meaning of sensational and understand how being sensational can help you attract customers, you need to think about how to apply sensational to your business.

Let's look at your business as though it's an apple.

If you think of an apple, there are basically three main parts: the skin of the apple, the fruit or the meat of the apple, and the core.

This apple is your business. Thinking in terms of your business, the skin is how everyone perceives you. It creates the first impression, and you must be sensational at that first point of contact.

The skin involves and contains your outward marketing. The skin is your external communication—the way your facility looks, your signage, advertising, outbound salespeople, uniforms, vehicles, and anything else the public sees. All of that is encompassed in the skin of the apple. It's the outward representation of your business to the world.

But then somebody walks through the doors or someone ends up on your web site, somebody initiates the buying process. They become a lead, it's almost like biting through that skin and now you're into the meat of the apple.

Now imagine you go to the store and you see the most beautiful apple, bright red, picture perfect. You take a bite out of it and it's lackluster. It has hardly any taste. It's just watery. It's mushy. It's grainy and has very little flavor. You were fooled by what was on the surface, and all you're left with is a bad taste in your mouth.

In the ideal scenario, when you bite into the apple, the inside is just as beautiful and tasty as the outside promised. So there's a congruency between what you communicate externally to the world and what the reality of doing business with your company is like. The consumption of your product or service must be as sensational as your outward appearance suggested it would be.

Finally, the core represents your core beliefs. It's what the owners, shareholders, managers, partners, and even the employees think about the business. This encompasses how you train your employees and what goes on behind closed doors.

For instance, think about a restaurant. You've got the sign outside the restaurant. You've got the dining room, and then you've got the kitchen and the bathroom. A restaurant can be judged on how clean its kitchen and bathrooms are. Typically in most restaurants, there's a nice dining area but the kitchen is a mess and you don't want to go back there.

Is the core of your business, your kitchen, sensational? Or is it just a facade on the outside and in the experience, but breaking down behind closed doors.

You could put a great message out there and orchestrate an excellent experience, but if deep down inside, the owner or the employees aren't on the same page when it comes to what the value proposition is, what the main goal of the company should be, what the mission, the vision, and core values are, then you're going to have a disconnect.

From the customers' standpoint, it's not going to be congruent and that leaves a bad taste in people's mouths. If you're going to have a company that is truly sensational and that customers gravitate to, it needs to be sensational on all levels: when the prospect experiences your outward communication; when your customer experiences the actual service or product; and how the owner, manager, and employees operate at the core of the company.

Frequently, we see a breakdown at one or all of the levels. Generally speaking, the biggest breakdown occurs from the outward communication to the consumption. In the past, when we worked for big advertising agencies, we dealt with a lot of automotive dealerships. The agency would come up with a potent, sensational campaign, and we would bring it to the table. The dealership would embrace it, and we would put it out there to the public. We'd come up with a great offer, a great concept, something fun, and we would put it out into the media. And people would experience that communication.

But when they would come off of the marketing into the dealership none of the salespeople would be aware of what the offer was or what the marketing was all about. The customers would be excited, and they would come in and say, "Tell me about this thing I heard on the radio or saw in the paper or saw on the television." And unfortunately the staff wouldn't know what they were talking about.

This is a major breakdown. It happens so frequently.

 From the Trenches

I went with my sister to shop for furniture for her new townhouse, recently. We came across this dining room table that she liked and wanted. Attached to the table was a tag that read "factory outlet clearance."

(continued)

It seemed like it might have been a floor model with an even deeper discount. When she indicated that she liked this table, the salesperson said, "Well, it will take six weeks to arrive because it's out of stock right now."

I pointed out the factory outlet clearance sign and asked if maybe this was the last of that particular model and if they were selling that actual table. The salesperson looked at the tag and said, "I don't know . . . I'm not sure what that tag means."

There it is, in the store, staring everyone right in the face. The salesperson must have walked past it a hundred times while she's doing business in the store. Yet she had no idea what it meant and had never bothered to ask or wonder.

There are several reasons this happens, but one of the main reasons is that there's a poison at the core. The consumption doesn't rot on its own.

It's always bad from the core out. This is why it's important for the business owner to be a master of the marketing. That marketing has to be congruent throughout the entire process: the outward marketing communication, the experience, the consumption, and the core. Marketing should be built for the consumption of the product and embraced at the core by the business owner herself and then communicated to all the employees and staff so everyone is on the same page and everyone understands what the purpose, mission and communication, and marketing plan is all about. That's how sensational works.

 From the Trenches

We once received an e-mail from a radio station alerting us that the station was receiving calls from listeners who had tried to call the advertiser (our client). The callers said the person answering the phones at our client's office didn't know anything about the offer mentioned in the ad.

Considering the high cost of advertising and the comparatively low cost of informing your staff, this seems like a pretty big no-brainer.

If you're running advertising, make sure everyone in your office is able to speak about it intelligently. The cost of a single lead can be huge for many companies, so a mistake can be very costly.

By the way, going a step beyond answering phones by knowing what is going on, including your employees in plans, and engaging them with information will yield more interested workers who will provide better service.

The Newton in All of Us

Become the Person Your Customers Revolve Around . . .

There are certain people in every industry who have managed to elevate themselves to expert or guru status. You probably know some in your industry.

Positioning yourself as an expert is essential to attracting customers. If you are an expert, marketing your business and your product or service becomes infinitely easier and less costly.

You read it right. If you are perceived as an expert, you won't need to spend as much on advertising and marketing. That's it.

The people screaming and yelling and putting pink gorillas on their roofs are trying to interrupt and divert people's attention. They're trying to prevent people from finding the experts.

They're afraid of experts because they aren't one. But just like you can't prevent water from running downhill, you can't prevent people from finding experts. People gravitate to experts. You will win the game if you are an expert.

Hopefully you've been reading this correctly and have grasped the huge potential that could come from positioning yourself as an expert.

Not only will you be able to worry less about advertising and marketing, but your profits will be bullet proof: your competition can undercut your prices, distribute coupons, and deeply discount their products and services and it *will not* affect your profit whatsoever.

How can this be possible? It's for real, and we're going to tell you how to do it.

This is information that most people have encountered personally without realizing its existence or its value. When we reveal this amazing strategy to you, you will feel infinitely more confident about your business and will even be able to charge significantly more than you have in the past for the same product or service.

This concept can increase your profits and make you more money this year, this month, or even this week.

Position yourself as an expert in your field. Become someone other people in your industry revolve around.

Becoming an expert in your field has many advantages in both your marketing and your business success. You will:

- Spend less on marketing and advertising.
- Have people seek you out.
- Have people talk about you and refer you to others.
- Have a higher perceived value in the marketplace.
- Be more respected by your customers and peers.
- Command higher prices for your products or services.
- Bullet proof yourself from competition.

How Do You Become an Expert?

That's a good question and before we can answer it, you have to answer these questions:

- Have you been working in your field longer than other people?
- Are you good at what you do?
- Do you know more about your business than the average person?
- Have you spent time educating yourself about your field of expertise?
- Are you confident in your ability to perform your job and service your customers?

If you answered yes, then you are already an expert. Congratulations.

Now, you need to position yourself as an expert in your field. Don't just say you're an expert, although this is a big first step. Most people aren't even doing that. But saying it isn't enough. You have to position yourself as the obvious expert in the minds and hearts of everyone you know.

Family, friends, customers, potential customers, and absolute strangers all must perceive you as the expert at what you do. Everyone likes to deal with the person who is the most knowledgeable on the subject, and if they feel that they are talking to that person, they aren't as concerned about prices.

Price concerns are a symptom of distrust, anxiety, and insecurity. Once you remove these factors from the buying process, the price objection ceases to exist.

Even better, you can actually charge more because people have been taught that they get what they pay for. It is not absurd to pay a bit more than the competitor's price if they are dealing with the expert.

Would clients of a local talent agency pay a bit more if they knew that the firm they were working with represented people like Brad Pitt? Of course they would. The clients would perceive that the firm has some sort of expert ability or can deliver a more expert opinion if it represents people they regard highly.

Positioning yourself as an expert takes a little effort. You have to eat, sleep, breathe, and live your expert perception. But you can't be an egomanic. This is the downfall of the whole process. You have to be genuine and interested in sharing what you know with people.

Experts give free advice all the time. They have a lot of it to give. But the advice has to be valuable or you're just spitting out junk.

Anyone can be a junk talker. You want to be the expert. Be interested in people and their problems. Offer help and encouragement and free advice when it comes to your field of expertise. Exploit this expert perception on everything and in everything you do.

You must exude expertise to be the expert. All your efforts should reinforce this: communication, marketing, advertising, web site, business cards, brochures, anything, and everything.

Positioning yourself as an expert doesn't take long. You just have to declare it to yourself and to the world. If you wait for someone else to anoint you as an expert, you will be waiting a long time.

Who appoints someone an expert anyway? A board of your competitors? Why would they ever want to make you an expert? So you can take all their business? It will never happen.

You have to leapfrog them. Appoint yourself the expert today and you will be one tomorrow.

Once you're an expert, you can command a higher level of respect from the people around you. This is critical. Suddenly, people will begin to listen to what you have to say. They'll get quiet when you begin to speak. Turning your expertise into free information and advice can allow you to leverage this newfound power into marketing success. Just make sure that you create action steps that prospects must take to earn your time and attention. We like to call this jumping through flaming hoops.

Do you see how as an expert you can turn the tables on the traditional vendor/customer relationship? Normally, you would have to earn your prospects' time and attention, but by positioning yourself as an expert to people who are interested in what you have to offer, you can make them come to you and earn your attention.

Here are some things you can do to rapidly build your own expert perception.

Write a Book

A book is an extremely powerful tool. In this country, we hold authors in very high regard. In fact, in many cases we automatically regard them as experts. Have you ever heard the saying, "He wrote the book on it?"

Authors go on tour, we go to their book signings, we want their autographs, we collect their works, and they get interviewed on radio and TV, and are featured in magazines and newspapers. Being an author and having a book carries a lot of weight and is something all aspiring experts should consider.

Imagine you are at a function and someone asks what you do. Instead of handing them a business card, you hand them your book. You immediately gain buckets of credibility. If the material is valuable, you gain tons more.

If you did it the traditional way, it would take a very long time to write a book, find a publisher, and then get it published. But you don't necessarily have to go through all of that.

Instead write a pamphlet, a small book, a white paper, a special report, or an industry bulletin and have someone edit it for you. If you doubt your ability as a writer, record yourself speaking and have the audio transcribed.

Having it professionally edited is important because you want it to look professional and be free of amateur grammar and spelling mistakes. You can find competent editors online for a reasonable fee.

You can have your finished product printed as a booklet or a book in no time for a few dollars per copy.

Another way to expedite the process is to use your web site as a tool to spread the word. Take your written material and create an e-book out of it. Have it available for free download on your web site.

$ Expert Resource

Raleigh Pinskey is the author of the international best-selling book, *101 Ways to Promote Yourself*. With over 100,000 copies in print, published in several languages, her book is the definitive guide on self-promotion. Raleigh speaks nationally on promotion and being an expert.

We told you that one of the B's in sensational is be more visible. Raleigh can show you how to "Maximize Your Biz-Ability Thru Viz-Ability."

To learn more about the power of increasing your visibility visit the Gravitational Marketing resource site at www.GravityBook.com/visible.

Write Articles

In addition to writing books and reports, you can write articles for newspapers, local publications, trade publications, and online e-zines. These are usually short 500 to 1,000 word pieces that give information on a very specific topic related to your industry or area of expertise.

Submit your articles to the editors of these publications, and let them know you are able to comment on these topics as an expert. Position yourself as a resource to them, and make yourself easily accessible to them all the time.

Clip and collect anything that you write that gets published. This is powerful fodder for your expert perception campaign and an invaluable sales tool.

Write a Newsletter

You can enhance your credibility as an expert by publishing a regular newsletter. Experts have things to say. Most other people do not. We recommend writing a newsletter monthly to ensure maximum impact.

What should you say? First of all, don't try to be overly technical or use industry jargon. In fact, you really don't need to talk about your industry at all. Most of your customers are not really interested in your industry. Instead, they're interested in the benefits they get from doing business with you. And if you position yourself as an expert and a celebrity, they'll be interested in you, too.

We recommend a mix of one-third business-related or how-to information, one-third emotional benefits, and one-third personal stories about your life.

Another powerful format is to stick to fun and interesting information. People are more likely to read a lighthearted newsletter filled with interesting facts than they are to read a technical newsletter that talks about the technology behind what you do or the industry you work in.

You should send your newsletter to all past and current customers as well as new leads whom you come in contact with. It's also helpful to send your newsletter to referral partners and centers of influence in your community or industry.

$	**Expert Resource**

Pete Lillo or, more aptly named, Pete The Printer, is the guy you want to know if your goal is to make more money from your existing customers (which we urge everyone to do). One of the biggest gold mines and sources of immediate cash in your business is your existing customer base. Most business owners simply don't utilize their existing customer base to its fullest.

Pete can automate the monthly newsletter strategy we discussed so it's ridiculously easy for you. He does all the work, and you reap the benefit of better relationships and a higher customer value.

To learn more about creating your own newsletter and how Pete can help you cash in on existing customers with his *Done4You* newsletter, visit the Gravitational Marketing resource site at www.GravityBook.com/newsletter.

Speak

Another great way to position yourself as an expert is to speak. Find local groups in your area or national organizations related to your field, and put together a presentation about your area of expertise. Make sure the content of the presentation is something people would be interested in hearing about.

Create a captivating title for the presentation that conveys the big benefit people will get from paying attention. Open the presentation with a list of things they will learn and what they will get when your talk is finished. Create an eagerness in them for what you have to say. Give them a way to get more information from you for free.

Some Places You May Be Able to Speak
- Chambers of Commerce.
- Civic clubs and organizations.
- Local association meetings.
- Business networking functions.
- Trade shows.
- Local universities, community colleges, and trade schools.
- National association meetings.

$ Expert Resource

Martin Howey, a man we like to call a friend, is a genius. He is responsible for helping thousands of people realize the full potential of their skills and talents by becoming business consultants. His consultants help small business owners take their companies to the next level and create uncommon success. He is the trainer's trainer. His wisdom and experience is unparalleled. Martin is the author of several books including *How to Start, Run, and Profit from Your Own 7-Figure Consulting Practice*. One of Martin's most powerful secrets is the use of endorsed mailings.

To learn more about how you can use your experience and expertise to help others, visit the Gravitational Marketing resource site at www.GravityBook.com/expert.

Host a Seminar

People like seminars and they carry a high, perceived value. If you have a complex product that people are interested in, you can host a free seminar. This is a great way to leverage your expert reputation and your time.

Let your local media know you are holding this seminar and create a press release about the event. Every bit of exposure helps, especially when it is free publicity.

The seminar should be created similarly to the presentation. The only difference is that the event is held in an environment of your choosing, it can be longer, and contain more hands-on learning and more content.

Make sure your books, reports, pamphlets, speeches, presentations, and seminars contain loads of valuable information to help prospects decide to become customers. Answer all the questions that you get from prospective customers and overcome typical sales objections.

Make your material fun to read or listen to. Don't be so dry and boring that people don't want to read your stuff or listen to your presentations. Make them interactive and interesting. Make them worth talking about to friends, relatives, and coworkers. This allows you to harness the power of word-of-mouth advertising and put it to work for you.

Don't hold back information for fear that people will steal your ideas or do it themselves. This happens infrequently and is not worth worrying about. The more you tell, the more you sell. That is the truth.

You are rewarded for the value you deliver to the marketplace. The more you give, the more you get in return.

The most important element of any free information is to offer a very clear and defined next step in the process. You don't want to leave anything to chance. This is the systematic process that people should follow to become your customers for life. You don't want them to have to figure it out on their own.

Lead them and they will follow. Give people an opportunity to get even more information from you—maybe in the form of buying your product or setting up a meeting with you to discuss their personal situation. Whatever it is, make sure it's easy to take the next step, and make sure you show them how to take it.

Collect their contact information, ask for their permission to give them more information as you create it, and build a database of prospects and customers. This information and database is the lifeblood of your future business. This concept is discussed in greater detail later in this book.

$ Expert Resource

You may be wondering, "How in the world will I be able to create all of this free information?" Printing and sending booklets, reports, CDs, and other valuable information widgets can be a confusing and time-consuming process. To master Gravitational Marketing, you need to do it—and do it well.

(continued)

Tony Wedel and his team at McMannis Duplication & Fulfillment have been a saving grace for us on many occasions. Why? They are the people who handle the printing, media duplication, packaging, and fulfillment of all of our expert information and physical products. They do a much better job than we could ever do ourselves.

If you want to get more customers and dramatically increase profits, then you need to remove yourself from the day-to-day task work and spend your time doing the things that grow your business. The problem is handing off the important work to a trustworthy, knowledgeable, and efficient firm. That's why we depend on the experts at McMannis Duplication & Fulfillment.

McMannis understands the Gravitational Marketing process, deadlines, and how to use information to attract prospects and presell them to your way of thinking. They have handled duplication, fulfillment, and marketing management for some of the top marketers in the country, including us.

They are industry experts at fulfilling multi-step marketing campaigns made up of printed and multimedia materials. CDs and DVDs are extremely powerful tools to attract and convert prospects into customers, leverage your time, and create more opportunities to have a life and business that are Enjoyable, Simple, and Prosperous.

To learn more about McMannis Duplication & Fulfillment and for additional tips on using information to position yourself as an expert and automatically enhance your sales process, visit www.GravityBook.com/duplication.

The Object of Your Attraction

Focusing Your Energy on the Perfect Prospects . . .

It doesn't matter how good your ads are, how good you are at selling, where you advertise, what you advertise, what your price is, or how much technology you've got piled up, you're not going to find much success in marketing if you don't aim at the right targets.

When judging an audience as a good or bad target for your product or service, one criteria to consider is whether they have already demonstrated a want for what you sell.

Let's talk about golfers who want to lower their score or increase the distance of their drive. They already want that improvement, and they will buy gadgets, gizmos, clubs, and all kinds of toys to get it. They've already demonstrated that. So if you're selling something to golfers, you don't want to go in and try to convince them that they should want something different. You wouldn't try to convince them that instead of wanting to lower their score or increase their drive they should want to be able to drive the golf cart faster. That's not what they want.

They've already demonstrated what they want, and if you're selling something that can deliver that benefit, then that's a good target for you because they already want what you offer. That's going to be your easiest sell. Those are going to be the easiest people to get to Gravitate to you.

This is about message-to-market match. Matching what you have to offer to the people who want to buy your product is the most important step. This is more than half of the marketing process. When you get this part right, when you match what you're selling to the people who want it, the process of marketing and selling is much easier and far more profitable. This is because people like to buy, even though they don't like to be sold.

If you can put something in front of them that gives them a benefit which they already, in their mind, know they want, you just say, "I know you want to increase the distance of your drive. Here's something that you could buy that will help you do that."—then they're going to be significantly more receptive to your sales message and your offer. Certainly more so than if you were to take a guy who wants to increase the distance of his drive and tell him that you have something that helps him to drive the golf cart faster. That's going to be a harder sell.

You should take all the benefits or solutions that your product can offer and match them to a group of people who are already thinking, "I want something that offers that benefit or solution." This will tie your product to their want.

Gravitational Targeting

> The definition of a target: Something or someone to be influenced or changed by an action or event.

Targeting is choosing the people you want to attract to your business or draw into your Gravitational Field. Your marketing is the action or event that causes this attraction. Targeting is often discussed but frequently ignored. It is critical to creating a successful marketing plan.

Randomly picking a target is unwise. Businesses can see wild success with the right target or fall flat on their faces with the wrong target. As much as 50 percent of the effectiveness of your marketing is a direct result of effective targeting.

Targeting requires discussion about who your potential customers really are. Since a major goal of Gravitational Marketing is to decrease your marketing expense while increasing effectiveness, it's important to define a target audience. This helps avoid costly waste associated with marketing to people outside your target.

To identify the *who* in your target, you must ask these three questions:

1. Who are you selling to?
2. Who is your best prospect?
3. Who is most likely to buy what you are selling?

For most businesses the answer should *not* be everyone.

We have found that most business owners don't focus enough time or attention on this step. Generally business owners like to jump right to the where-do-I-put-my-ad step in the process. Without spending adequate time researching and choosing a target, all of your other efforts are pointless and most of your dollars are wasted.

Many businesses, entrepreneurs, and salespeople we consult with are frightened by the concept of narrowing and targeting. They think that if they only focus on a certain small group of people, they will end up missing out on a large portion of the business they could have gotten. This is bad logic.

In business, you cannot be all things to all people. If you try, you will get nothing for your efforts. Businesses and salespeople who try to cover all the bases and offer products that solve every ailment are destined to be ignored by the marketplace.

Americans are exposed to thousands of marketing messages per day and we have become very astute at ignoring them. To get attention from prospects, you have to be for them, not for everyone. People believe a solution for the masses is for the masses, not for them. If your marketing is too broad, you will be ignored. Targeting and creating products geared specifically for that target is the only route to success.

Defining Your Target

Most businesses can't consider the entire population of the world as potential prospects. The people who have access to your product are called your *universe*. A universe can be as big as the population of the world or as small as a five-mile radius around your business.

What Determines Your Universe?

Your distribution, resources, and type of business determine your universe. If you are a local business that sells sporting goods, your universe is a lot smaller than the universe of Nike. Your universe is the area where your product can be sold and you can adequately service your customers.

Let's say you are a local small business that only services and sells to customers within a five-mile radius of your location. Your universe becomes all of the people living in that five-mile radius. But if you can serve customers from around the country, the entire country is your universe.

The all-important question is, "Is everyone in that universe your target?" The simple answer to that question is, "Probably not."

Unless you have a product or service that is likely to be purchased by most people in the world, country, or in a five-mile radius and unless you have a marketing budget stout enough to reach all of those people, you'll need to narrow it down.

Narrowing your universe is the first step in targeting. There are three main ways in which you can slice your universe into manageable targets:

1. Geographic targeting.
2. Demographic targeting.
3. Categorical targeting.

Geographic Targeting

Narrowing your universe by distance, zip code, area, or location is the key to geographic target marketing. If you own an ice cream parlor in Charleston, West Virginia, people in Charleston, South Carolina, are not your potential prospects. Even people in the next town over aren't your prospects.

You have to ask yourself who your potential prospects are. Start by considering all of your points of purchase. These questions will help you apply a geographic filter to your potential prospects:

- Do you have multiple locations in your city or town?
- Do you have locations in multiple towns?
- What effective range does your business have?
- How far will people travel to come to you?
- How far will you travel to go to them?
- Do licensing or compliance issues exist that limit the area?

If you can only do business in a small, fixed, geographic area and you have a relatively broad appeal, such as a real estate agent, lawn service, or restaurant, you may be able to rely solely on geographic targeting.

Some real estate agents can provide great examples of geographic target marketing. When an agent uses geographic targeting they call it *farming*. When an agent farms a geographic target area, they hit everyone in that area with mail, flyers, events, newsletters, door-to-door solicitation, bandit signs, and sponsorships. They use a total domination strategy, but only to that specific geographic area. They do not focus on anyone else outside the area.

Geographic targeting is the most basic and easiest form of target marketing, and for some businesses, selling products or services with a broad appeal in a small area with a small distribution and a small budget, it works fine.

But what if your business doesn't fit that profile? Then you need to seek a more narrow targeting strategy.

Demographic Targeting

Geography isn't the only limiting factor that you have at your disposal. You know your business better than anybody else. If you own a steakhouse, vegetarians are not likely to dine at your restaurant. If you own a solar pool heating company, people without pools are not potential prospects. If you manage a house painting business, apartment dwellers are not good potential prospects.

Demographics is all about data. The more information you can get about the people who buy your product or service, the better you will be able to use demographic targeting to find more of them.

What if you don't have a product or service that already has customers you can profile? Look at your competitors and see who is buying their products, then analyze their customers. Things to look for when analyzing a group of people for demographic targeting are:

- What is their income?
- What is their net worth?
- Do they have investments?

- Do they have and use credit cards?
- What magazines do they read?
- Do they rent or own their home?
- Do they have pets?
- Do they have a family?
- Do they travel?
- Do they buy products by mail?

If your product isn't for everyone and most really should not be, you need to start characterizing your prospects and customers by their demographic information. Compile this information; figure out who your best customers are, where they live, and how to reach them. Then spend your money marketing only to those people.

Combining Geographic and Demographic Targeting

If your local business has a specialty product or service, then you need to combine both geographic and demographic targeting to narrow your local universe into a very specific group of people. For example, say you own a mobile pet grooming business, and you know that you don't want to travel more than 10 miles to trim a dog, so you use geographic targeting to narrow your universe. But you also know that people who don't own dogs aren't good prospects, so you use demographic targeting to narrow your list even more. Finally, you end up with a list of dog owners in a 10-mile radius around your business. This highly targeted group of people contains your best prospects.

If you are on a limited marketing budget, it is best to start with the narrowest target possible and then broaden your target as you dominate that market. Never start with a broad target and a small budget; that is the code for disaster in any marketing effort.

Categorical Targeting

Categorical target marketing is about putting people into groups that either have an association with you or with each other. Some examples of this would be:

- Occupation/Industry.
- Social groups.
- Clubs.
- Civic or professional organizations.
- Fraternities or sororities.
- Trade associations.
- Alumni associations.
- Hobbies.

Categorical targeting allows you to narrow your focus to people who have something in common with each other, similar interests with one another and quite likely with you. This can be powerful because it allows you to cater your marketing message to those commonalities or interests and speak the language of your prospects. Categorical targeting provides an excellent opportunity for building a relationship with a high degree of trust and rapport.

Choosing the Right Target

Once you've narrowed your target and you know exactly who it is that you want to get your message in front of, you have to test it and make sure that it is a viable one. There are three critical questions you need to ask yourself about the target you chose:

1. Have people in this target shown an interest or desire for what I have to offer?
2. Do people in this target spend money on items or services like I offer?
3. Are people in this target easy to reach?
4. If the answer to all of these questions isn't *yes* then you need to rethink your target.

A Starving Crowd

Is your target hungry for what you are offering? Is your target a starving crowd waiting for someone to give them something to satisfy their hunger pangs, wants, and desires? It better be or you're in trouble.

The most important part of this whole process is that you define your target market and then forget about the people who don't fall inside of it. Don't waste another dollar intentionally advertising to them. Instead, start considering methods to specifically reach those people within your target. Save your marketing dollars and your gravity for a better use. This is the start of a successful marketing strategy.

Reasons You Should Create a Better Target

Let's discuss the 13 overwhelming reasons you should create a better target.

Save Money

Targeting prevents you from wasting money talking to people who aren't hungry for what you have to offer.

Save Time

Targeting also saves you time. If you monkey around with a general one-stop-shop message or product, you're wasting a great deal of time. You have to answer this question for yourself. If you're the type of person who, at the end of the week, has completely run out of time, hasn't gotten the things done that she needed to get done, and hasn't gotten to spend enough time with her family, then you are probably wasting precious time because of your failure to identify an appropriate target. When you identify the right target, you stop wasting time, money, and resources marketing to people who aren't good prospects.

Sell Easier

If you have an effective target, selling becomes easier because you know exactly who your prospects are, where they are, and what they want.

When you niche yourself as the perfect solution for a narrow target, you will have very little competition. Because so few people target, you end up being in a class by yourself.

Create a Clear Message

It makes creating a message easier. If you find yourself writing a script for a cold call, sales meeting, or presentation and you end up staring at the paper stumped, you probably don't have a defined target. When you know your target, things become crystal clear for you. You know what to say because you know what they want to hear. You know what the hot buttons are that make your target prospects tick. That's what you talk about. You talk about what they want and the way they feel. You get inside their head, feel their pain, and offer them a solution.

Get Referrals

It makes getting referrals easier. When you have a clearly targeted message that resonates with your audience it makes word-of-mouth advertising happen automatically. If your target prospects experience the positive benefits of the solution your product or service delivers, then it is much easier for those people to talk about you. Most likely, their friends are part of the target too—remember, birds of a feather flock together. If you have an understandable targeted message and your customers are receiving a great benefit from your product or service, they will spread the message to their friends and family who are also likely prospects. When the message is clear and easily under-standable, word of mouth travels faster. When word of mouth travels faster, your business grows faster. This results in spending less money on marketing and advertising.

Get Employee Buy In

It helps employees understand their mission and roles better. Many companies struggle with this. If you have a company with employ-ees and the company isn't well targeted, many of your employees may spend a good portion of their time wondering exactly what it is they are doing. They may waste time searching for focus. This can really affect your sales staff negatively. They may be wasting time trying to determine the target and come up with a targeted message on their own. Hopefully they get it right, but most likely they are confused and without direction. Productivity and morale are impacted when employees have no clearly defined purpose. This is what a target provides.

Be an Expert

Effective targeting allows you to become an expert and specialist. You're not trying to be an expert on everything and for everyone. By narrowing your target, you can specialize in something very specific and more easily position yourself as an expert. Think of medical specialists. The top experts are those who specialize in something very specific, like infant neurology, trauma-related hip fractures, or ocular disease due to diabetes. The list goes on and on.

Command a Higher Price

Effective targeting allows you to command a higher price. If you target well, you can dominate your competition and charge more. For instance, rather than being a run-of-the-mill disc jockey, you could become a disc jockey for corporate banquets. Most disc jockeys are going to find jobs at weddings, Bar/Bat Mitzvahs, and Sweet Sixteen parties. They go wherever they need to for the work. But if you become the disc jockey specialist in corporate banquets, it's quite likely that you'll be able to command a higher price. Customers will pay more because you are an expert and specialist and can demand more for that expertise.

Eliminate the Competition

With good targeting, there is less comparison and competition. When you have a very tightly defined target, it's harder to be compared to the competition. If there's no one else offering what you're offering, you are in a class by yourself. Again, let's go back to the disc jockey offering his expertise as a corporate banquet specialist. When prospects compare him to the general disc jockey, the two sales pitches don't look anything alike. It really becomes a no-brainer, and the specialized disc jockey ends up with more business and more money per transaction.

The specialist has less competition. Prospects can't compare, so the specialist can command a higher price and be viewed as an expert, which creates a sales process with less hassle.

Create a Better Product

Effective targeting allows you to create a better product or service. If you've defined a narrow target, you're not trying to create something for everybody. Now you can focus on what you really do, rather than trying to be all things to all people.

Let's say you provide ink jet and toner refills. This is a pretty big business with lots of competition. Basically it's a fierce, price-driven market. But let's say that you could specifically cater your service to law offices. You would say, "I know law offices use an absurd amount of toner and ink because they go through so much paperwork. Rather than focusing on everybody, I'm going to build my service completely around law offices. I'm going to install some features that most of my competitors don't have. Most of my competitors probably charge $40 for a toner refill and drop it off. Instead, I get to know my target specifically and learn some things that could really help their business. I understand the unique and distinct pains the attorneys and their office staff have, and I cater my service around them specifically."

You wind up with a better quality service for the law offices, which goes back to a higher price, with less comparison. In addition, if you niche yourself as a toner and ink refill company for law offices, you could create a national business right out of your local office. You could ultimately grow your prospect list exponentially. You could drastically expand your marketplace just by thinking a little differently.

You may think you're giving up too much of the market. You have to take that risk. You have to give up some to get more. That's the concept of targeting. Actually, because you are targeting, because you are limiting yourself, you can command a higher price and have less competition. You become a specialist. You have a better product or service, and you can speak the prospect's language.

Tell Your Story

Targeting allows your business to have a better story for the press. Articles written about your business carry seven times the weight of an ad. This is because articles are more believable and credible. Given this, it should be a goal for every business to be written about or to get press.

An easy way to do that is to have a worthwhile story to tell. A one-stop shop is not an exciting story for any writer. But a company with a narrow target becomes a very interesting tale. There is an automatic press opportunity built in when you target. It is not the norm, therefore, it is more interesting.

There are probably publications that cater to the same markets you cater to. Look at newsstands. Look at magazines racks at the bookstore. How many magazines are there? You'll see there are hundreds. Those magazines aren't for the general population. They are each for a specially targeted group of people. There is probably a publication out there that caters to your specific market. They are always looking to write about things their readers are interested in. They need stories and if you have targeted your business then your product may be something they'd be interested in.

We're not talking about publications for the general population. The odds of getting picked up in some of those big publications are very slim, besides, their readers are not your target. If you are targeting a specific group of people, the odds of getting mentioned in a publication written only for them are very high.

We have clients who have had articles written about them in these niche magazines. They have received calls from their write-ups even five to seven years after the actual stories ran. They found a starving crowd, found a way to speak directly to them, and offered them something they really wanted.

Dominate Your Target

When you know exactly who you're trying to reach, who your customers are, and you've created your service around that target, you can dominate that target. This is possible because you know exactly who they are, where they are and what they want. When you give them exactly what they want and you are the only one offering it to them, you get massive amounts of business.

Specialize Your Products

Every business is more likely to appeal to a narrower group of people than it would to everyone. In other words, you're more likely to have a greater appeal to a small group than you will have to a large group. In our opinion, this is the most important and telling benefit of all.

People want to feel like the products and services they buy are specialized and specially designed for them. Any given product or service will always have a group of people with an affinity for it. Everyone else will probably be indifferent or not like it.

It goes back to the rule of thirds. Wouldn't it be great to have one third of the audience dying to buy your product, rather than having no one interested at all? There will always be people who could care less about your product, but the goal is to reach those who will care about it. You want to make it speak directly to them. You do this by creating your product or service especially for them to meet their wants and desires.

Penalties of Poor Targeting

Waste

Poor targeting wastes time and money talking to people who don't matter. People who aren't interested will never buy. So, you need to stop wasting your time and money marketing to them. Time and money are your most valuable resources. There are better ways to use them.

Burnout

You burn out your sales staff with poor targeting. Perhaps you are burnt out yourself. You or your sales staff are probably making sales calls, doing all that manual sales bull-work. You're running yourself ragged. You're spinning your wheels. You're burning up shoe leather, and you're thinking you can't get anywhere. Most likely it's because you don't have a good target. You're not sure who you're talking to.

Competition

You're forced to compete as a commodity. Do you deal with this in your business? People tell us, "I've just got to lower my price. There are other companies that have lower prices, so I can't compete." These types of people are not perceived as experts, so how could they charge more? You don't have to compete as a commodity when you target properly.

Invisibility

You aren't really worth talking about. This may seem harsh. But one of the worst penalties for being untargeted is that no one talks about you. That is an awful place to be. You don't have a great story because you're just for the general public. You're for everyone. You're boring. And if you are boring, you are invisible. No one knows who you are, and no one sees you if you don't stand out. If it's hard to understand who your products are for, it's hard for people to recommend you to other people. You receive no word-of-mouth advertising or press.

Tools for Researching a Potential Target Market

Now that you understand targeting and why it is so important, let's discuss some online spy tools you can use to research a potential target market.

Overture Inventory to Keyword Research

The web site http://adlab.msn.com monitors keyword activity on the Web. The keyword forecast tool shows you the keyword search volume over a period of time and predicts the future search activity of that keyword.

Even if you're not considering advertising online, this is powerful. Even if you don't have a web site or a reason to discuss the Internet, this is still very important.

Get on the computer and go to this site with a list of 10 or 20 words that describe your business. Plug them into this tool. You may be shocked at what you find.

If you know the number of times a particular term that's related to your business is searched, you can determine the level of interest that exists out there for that term. The number of times the words related to your potential target market are searched worldwide in a given month is indicative of the level of interest the population has for that concept.

Here are some more quick ways you can use this. You can gauge whether anyone cares about what you're talking about to begin with. The keyword group detection tool tells you similar searches that people are doing. This means there is another way to describe your business that you may not have thought of, that other people are using. It gives you new language and a new vernacular to use when talking to your target. This is very important because you want to speak in their language.

eBay

Another online targeting tool can be found at www.ebay.com. Lots of people buy on eBay. They buy all sorts of things. You can find anything and everything on eBay. It's great for people with unique interests to buy hard-to-find items.

Using eBay, you can determine if people have an ability and willingness to spend money on what you have to offer. If they're selling it on eBay and people are buying, there is interest.

Of course, whether this is a good tool for you depends on what kind of products you're selling. This doesn't work for everybody. If you look at the categories on the eBay web site, there are all sorts of products such as digital cameras, sporting goods, electronics, even clothing.

If you can find a category that your product would fit in, you can open up that category on their web site. First of all, you will see the top 10 items selling in that category. What are the hot items? Does your product happen to be one of them? Or, is it similar to one of them? That will tell you if there's a buying frenzy over what you're offering or if something like what you're offering is hot. If it's hot on eBay, that's a good sign that people are interested and willing to spend money.

Keep in mind that eBay can also give you a false negative, meaning that just because what you offer isn't on eBay doesn't mean that it's not valuable or salable. It's not the final word, it's just helpful.

Amazon

Another place to look is www.amazon.com. Amazon is great for determining the interest level of a target. If people are writing and buying books on a topic for the target you are thinking about, then that demonstrates an interest and willingness to spend money by that target.

For instance, if someone publishes a book about professional techniques in pet and animal photography and people are buying it, then there must be some interest in that market. You know people will buy pet photography products.

Another great way to use Amazon is to locate the top sellers and examine the language that's used. You're looking for the titles and the tone. You might want to buy a couple of the top sellers and read them.

You want to mimic that tone for your audience because whatever's selling best right now represents the conversation that's already going on in people's heads. Another extension of that is to find the appeals that are used in the titles of the best sellers.

This gives you an idea of the language that is being used for successful selling right now. And if you happen to find a book in the top sellers list that is related to the target you're considering, that's more positive proof that you're on a good track. It's a conversation that's already going on inside the heads of the public and hopefully your target. If you can relate your message back to that existing conversation, you'll find great success.

Reaching Your Target

It's important to realize that unless at least one of these conditions exists, you're not going to be able to reach your target, which makes it a bad choice. At least one of the following four things must exist.

Internet Searches

Check searches on the Internet. Ask yourself: Does my target have a problem that they can describe, and do they believe that they can find a solution for it on the Internet? Are they currently searching for that solution?

You will only be able to reach your target online if they believe they can find a solution to their problem on the Internet and if they are already searching for it online. If they are, then you can use the Internet to reach your target.

Print

Look at print publications. Are there publications written specifically for your target that your target reads regularly? If there's a niche publication that your target reads, then you will be able to reach that target in that publication.

Mail

If you're a do-it-yourselfer, head down to the library, and look at a copy of the *Standard Rate and Data Service* (SRDS). You could also subscribe to it online for around $600 a year. You could also call a list broker to get help with it.

You should look for a particular list that matches your target. For instance, imagine you are a pet photographer like we talked about earlier. You might decide, after profiling your customers, that you want to reach people who have purchased pet products via mail in the past 60 days in your area, who also have two kids, own their own vehicle, and have credit cards. You could use SRDS to find out if there's a list available that matches that.

You can always find out who has credit cards, who owns a vehicle, who has kids, but the real question is can you find a list of people who have bought pet products in the past 60 days by mail? Most likely the answer is yes. But that's why you want to look at SRDS or talk to a list broker. If the answer is yes, then you know that you can easily reach those people via direct mail.

Sometimes, if you have a small geographic target and you try to do that kind of specific demographic and categorical targeting, you may end up running into very small list quantities. You've got to be careful about that.

Be prepared. You're going to pay more money for those names when you start. This is because the list broker will have to merge and purge many different lists with your criteria to get exactly what you want.

You could also go directly to the niche magazine for lists. For example, you could go to a dog owner's magazine and buy a local subscriber list that contains the names of dog enthusiasts in your area.

> Any dollar spent on better list segmenting is always returned in results.

Associations

The final way to discover if you can reach your target is through associations. Are there associations that represent your target? Do these associations have a magazine or newsletter? Do they have a trade show or convention? If they do, then most likely you can be involved in those things. You can reach your target prospects that way. If they have an association, it's a great indicator that they'll be reachable and that you'll have a way to talk to them.

A Shortcut to Targeting

Let's discuss how your existing business can use this information to choose a target or niche and move forward with it.

The first thing you want to do is examine your customer base carefully. Look for commonalities and trends. The information is there. You just need to know how to sort through it. Profile your customer base. Determine the preferable group of customers. You may want to look at who purchases one of your products or services that has a good profit margin built into it.

Imagine you're a financial planner. You know you help seniors, business owners, young single executives, and families trying to save to send their kids to college. You have a very broad target. You're probably finding it difficult to get leads.

First of all, you need to go through all your clients and determine where most of your customers come from. Do you have a majority of senior clients? If so, that may be a good market on which to focus.

Maybe they're all equal. In that case, you should ask yourself these questions: Which group do I like working with best? Which group gives me a higher net profit? Which group gives me more referrals? Which group comes back to me more often? Which group is going to be a customer longer?

The commonalities aren't always obvious. They're not necessarily age, income, credit cards, or car ownership. They could be odd personal traits that you couldn't even find out on paper. They could be things that you would only know by watching the people.

Sometimes those distinguishing characteristics say a lot about who the person is. If the customers who buy the most from you all drive European cars or all wear Brooks Brothers suits, then you've uncovered some very valuable information for targeting. People in the same target tend to flock together, so it isn't weird if you find they have similar traits. If you can determine what those are, then you can find a way to get lists of those people and have greater success.

From the Trenches

I was reading a recent edition of *Advertising Age*, an industry publication for us advertising nutcases, and there was an interesting story I thought I'd share with you.

The story was about the battle between Burger King and their National Franchisee Organization. The two organizations were fighting over pricing and promotion plans, including the chain's $340 million dollar ad budget.

Their ad campaign had been working marvelously. Same-store sales rose 6.8 percent last year, the best performance in over a decade for the burger giant. But last quarter's numbers weren't as good, only a 1.1 percent same-store sales gain.

So now franchisees are starting to voice their displeasure. What's their main beef? Is the campaign too narrowly focused?

Most of Burger King's profit comes from the target—male teens. So the agency built the "The King," "Dr. Angus," "Subservient Chicken," "Coq Roq," and other wild campaigns.

The campaigns have gotten massive attention in this demographic but some franchisees are concerned that they are missing out on other segments of the population, like the female market that McDonald's is focusing their efforts on.

Are the franchisees right?

Is focusing your $340 million dollar ad budget on the specific portion of the population that represents the largest profit center for your company a smart move? I would have to say absolutely *yes*!

It doesn't surprise me that the franchisees would want to be all things to all people. That is a common mistake among business owners who don't take the time to learn the basics of the most important part of their business—marketing.

You must pick a target and stick to it. Be for them absolutely. Make them love you. Identify them, follow them, grow with them, and change as they do. Be fast and agile. Burger King is doing that and it has proven successful for them for the first time in a decade.

None of the franchisees are in the target demographic, so none of them *get* the commercials. They don't like them. They're not supposed to. The commercials aren't for them.

But their ego is getting in the way. They want to like the commercials. They want to give them their stamp of approval. They think they know everything.

(continued)

A lot of business owners are this way. Entrepreneurs have big egos. It's part of being an entrepreneur. But entrepreneurs who find true success and wealth are the ones who can put their egos aside and surround themselves with people who know more about the subjects they themselves aren't uniquely and 100 percent qualified to do.

For every point of ego you add to your marketing, subtract one point of effectiveness. Many ads are 100 percent ego driven, and so, they fail 100 percent.

Increase Your Gravitational Potential

Supercharging Your Attractability . . .

When someone sets out to buy your product or service they have a thousand other options. Why in the world would they choose you?

If you're thinking about starting a business, if you already own a business, or if you're a sales professional, you may have already asked yourself this question. Or maybe you haven't.

Whatever the case, ask yourself now. Why would someone choose you?

Why Do People Buy?

Perhaps we should begin with a discussion of why people buy in the first place. Have you ever thought about that? Why do people buy from you? Why do people buy anything?

If you think about it for a moment, you can probably come up with some or all of the right answers.

First, let's focus on the wrong answers. It's important to identify the wrong answers so that you can begin the process of eradicating them from your life.

The reasons people don't buy are just as important as the reasons they do. Bad things happen when you expect people to buy for the wrong reasons, such as—they don't buy anything.

Getting people to buy a product or service generally costs money and/or time. That's sales/marketing/advertising.

If you ignore the psychology behind the buying process, you make your job tougher thereby costing more time or money or both.

By ignoring the true reasons that motivate people to buy, you're going against the current. It seems elementary, but we can't stress this point enough.

The truth is that most companies ignore the basic principles that cause people to buy. They're pushing a rope uphill. Over the years, we've been ingrained with the wrong ideas. Most companies are just in the herd trying to imitate what they see on television.

If you can erase these hardwired concepts from your brain, your job will be much easier. By digging beneath the surface, finding what truly motivates your customers and exploiting the information, the task of marketing will be like sailing with the wind instead of into it.

Wrong Answer 1: Chance

Chance is the primary marketing method used by many companies. Prepare your product or service, buy an ad in the phone book, light up the sign, and wait for the people to come to you.

Have you tried this? Some people have success with this method. Some people win in Vegas. If that's you, then congratulations are in order.

For the rest of us, chance just won't cut it.

Too many people still aren't sure how to control their customers or don't think they have the money to do it properly. They say, "Hopefully our customers will realize our [insert product here] is better than our competitors'."

Chances are, people will never realize that, and even if they do business with you once, the majority may never come back to you. Why should they? All you did was roll the dice to begin with.

It's natural for some customers to end up doing business with you by chance. Consider it manna from heaven. But don't depend on it.

What elements of chance exist in your business? Identify them, and refuse to depend on them. Soon, you'll have significantly better methods at your disposal.

Wrong Answer 2: Price

Most people and most business owners incorrectly believe that a low price is a powerful tool to get people to buy. The truth is that price is very easily controlled. Almost any businessperson, skilled or not, can control the price of their product or service. That's why it's so often used as a marketing tool.

But lowering your price comes with a price. The obvious problem is that you make less for doing the same work you did before. It cuts right into your profit.

Of course, for very large companies low price can be a powerful tool. They can use low prices to become a giant and to dominate their marketplace. When you're selling that kind of volume, having a small net profit on many products (or no net on some others) can still yield big profits. Surely one discount chain comes to mind.

When you lower your price, it often serves only to devalue your product or service. That's the opposite of your ultimate goal. If you are a smart marketer, your goal should be to build the value of your product—not decrease it. But that doesn't stop companies everywhere from trying to outprice their competition to get business.

Sometimes, price may not even be an objection. If price isn't what's keeping your potential customers from buying, what will lowering the price accomplish? Not much.

Price concerns only arise when the customer is having difficulty associating appropriate value with the offering. Your job is to increase the value not decrease the price. There's a big difference.

While price is sometimes a contributing factor in the motivating process, it's not a positive factor you can count on.

It can ultimately lead to you doing more work for less money (or no money) while devaluing your product—and it may not even do anything positive for you. Do yourself a favor; don't mess with your prices (unless you raise them). That's not the real reason people buy anyway.

Wrong Answer 3: Advertising

Advertising can be an enormously powerful tool for influencing people to come to your store, purchase your product or service, or identify themselves as being interested in what you offer.

But it is only a tool. It's a vehicle for communicating your message. Advertising without an effective reason doesn't work. Typical advertising efforts only serve to get your name out there and that doesn't affect a prospect's desire to buy.

Don't make the mistake of expecting your advertising or marketing alone to make the difference in your business. Instead you must only expect advertising to help you sift and sort your audience so that you can determine who is a prospect and who is not.

Now, let's discuss the real reasons people buy.

Correct Answer 1: High Return on Investment

> There are thousands of ways for your prospects to waste their money these days. Don't be one of them.

Strive to offer a truly outrageous return on your customer's investment. This means that whatever money they spend for your product or service should be outweighed by the value they receive in return. They should finish their transaction with you feeling like they got a good deal.

Prospects will reward you for having a high return on investment (ROI) offering. Anything less and you'll have to resort to less-than-ethical tactics to move your product or service.

It may be helpful to envision a woodchopper and his assistant. Imagine the woodchopper chopping away, splitting logs and piling the split logs in his assistant's arms. Eventually the assistant would collapse under the weight of all those logs. Now imagine those split logs were value in the form of expert information, bonus gifts, additional services, and the like. Eventually your prospect will collapse under the weight of all that value. That's what you should aspire to. Transform your offering into something so valuable that your prospect collapses under the weight, gives in, and buys.

Correct Answer 2: Emotional Benefits

Some people buy solely for emotional reasons. Then they back up their emotional decisions with an attempt at logic. Typically, they can create a logical argument to support any emotional decision—no matter how ridiculous.

Have you ever splurged on a purchase that you knew you couldn't afford? What happens next? You begin rationalizing all the reasons you made a good decision. That rationalization helps you sleep at night. But it was the overcharged emotions that made you buy in the first place.

What emotions do your product or service arouse?

A few popular and driving emotional factors (we call these *G-forces* because of their effect on a company's Gravitational Potential):

- Pain.
- Greed.
- Hope.
- Relief.
- Joy.
- Safety.
- Belonging.

People are searching for relief from or achievement of all of these emotions. When people buy anything other than bare necessities (basic clothing, food, shelter), they are buying based on emotions like these.

Think about it. We could all live on bread, water, grass, and bananas. We could live in a modest apartment with minimal costs per month. For that matter, we could live in mud huts. We could drive an old vehicle that only serves to get us from point a to point b or we could ride a bike. We could wear burlap bags for clothing and wear old tire remnants on our feet for shoes.

That's not how we live, and it's probably not how you live either. Why? Because the other niceties of our life like tasty food, fancy homes, luxurious cars, and designer clothing fulfill the emotional desires we have—the desire for joy, the desire to belong, the desire for relief from pain and greed. This is the difference between need and want. People buy what they want, not always what they need.

Here are the 12 things most people want out of life:

1. House and home.
2. Status.
3. Job security.
4. Health.
5. Money.
6. Good looks.
7. Personal and family life.

8. Security.
9. Vitality.
10. Valued possessions.
11. Friends.
12. Sex appeal.

To carry this subject further (which we will because it's that important), every motivation can be driven by the needs found on Maslow's hierarchy of needs (see Figure 6.1).

Because the pyramid represents a hierarchy, it is important to note that the higher on the pyramid you go, the higher the level of desire and the lesser the level of need.

The need for air will always win out over the need to feel fulfilled. But the desire to be fulfilled preys on the mind more then the need for air.

FIGURE 6.1   Maslow's Hierarchy of Needs. Maslow's hierarchy has a major impact on all marketing campaigns. The basic needs and desires outlined here are the foundation for any buying preference and sales transaction. Although not often considered important in business and marketing, Maslow's hierarchy of needs should be hanging on the wall of anyone interested in naturally attracting customers.

Notice that the emotional factors listed earlier all have a place on this pyramid. Find the ones that fit your prospects best and push those buttons.

If people are emotionally attached to your product, they will buy your product. But why would someone ever be emotionally committed to a product or a service? They wouldn't be.

The emotional commitment comes from people's fears or desires and your ability to resolve or deliver them.

People are committed to the unique emotional benefits that your product or service offers them. They are emotionally committed to a dream, a wish, a hope, a vision of the absence of some pain or the presence of some gain that they have mentally created, that your product or service makes possible.

It is this dream, wish, hope, or vision that makes them buy. You must uncover your prospects' emotional desires—the things that keep them up at night in anticipation or anxiety—then your product or service must create an unyielding link to the realization of those emotional factors so that they can create a euphoric reality around the benefits it offers.

Selling to an emotional hot button lessens the occurrence of buyer's remorse or unhappy customers. And when your product or service strikes an emotional chord that is great enough, price becomes a nonissue.

You will have strong relationships with customers who are emotional about what you do and who are not concerned with price. So, in that regard, emotion is the reciprocal of price as a sales tool. Don't lower your price; increase your emotional appeal.

$	**Expert Resource**

Craig Garber is known as the King of Copy. He's an attraction expert and personal friend. His brash, pull-no-punches style is a breath of fresh air for us and a real-life example of the Rule of Thirds in action.

Craig knows more about pushing the emotional buy buttons of prospects than anyone we know. And fortunately for you, he has put everything he knows down on paper into his trademarked system called Seductive Selling®. We personally own this system and can tell you with certainty, if you want to motivate prospects to take action, this system will give you an advantage over your competition.

To learn more about how to push your prospects' buy buttons and convert more of the leads you attract, visit the Gravitational Marketing resource site at www.GravityBook.com/seductive.

Correct Answer 3: Believability

Delivering a high ROI offering and uncovering emotional triggers are huge steps in attracting potential customers and making them emotionally committed to you and what you have to offer.

But there is one critical piece of the puzzle that we haven't discussed: Believability, also known as, "Why should I believe you?"

The easiest way to rapidly create believability is expert positioning.

People truly want to do business with experts. In the sea of choices that people have, there are dozens or scores or hundreds of companies out there yelling and screaming about their features ... beating their chests about the benefits (if they have figured that part out).

But almost nobody positions himself or herself as an expert. They can beat their chests all day, but when people find out about a real, live expert they can have access to, they won't even dream of going to anyone else.

Another very big bonus—people talk about experts, people ask experts to speak, people read experts' books, people recommend experts to their friends because it makes them feel important.

From the Trenches

Oh my goodness, you wouldn't believe the difficulty I had choosing a Christmas gift for my mom.

I had chosen her name in our family gift exchange. And I knew she wanted a new Bluetooth wireless headset for her cell phone.

The problem was I didn't know anything about them. That is rarely the case with me and technology but these gizmos have not captured my interest.

So I went shopping, and to my dismay, nobody else seemed to know anything either.

Frankly, I would have gladly bought the best one on the shelf (it's for my mom after all), but I couldn't figure out which one was the best or why one was worth more than another.

I began by comparing packages at multiple stores. None of the packaging made any sense. Not one package gave me a clear, compelling reason to buy or explained the unique benefits I would find with that particular model.

Instead, I got a bunch of technical jargon and esoteric features I didn't understand.

How about: better sound quality than model X, longer battery life than brand Y, more durable than the previous model—anything, something.

But every model between $50 and $150 seemed exactly the same. There had to be some difference. The store clerks seemed to know less than the package.

One clerk told me they were pretty much all the same. So why spend the $150? What's the difference?

I was *desperate* for a buying preference. I wanted some reason to choose one over the other. I have a feeling I wasn't alone this season. It's a common mistake made by big companies.

The real danger comes when smaller companies decide to model their sales or marketing techniques after the big companies. When your product or service begins to look like all the others with no discernable difference, price becomes the only variable. And the lowest price wins. That's a bad situation to be in.

You can break out of the price mold by delivering a clear and compelling buying preference. That's all people really want.

Sure, people want a good deal, and they think they want a low price. But if you built more value into one choice and raised the price, many people would splurge. People want the best. It's only when there is no perceivable *best* that they resort to price.

But too many business owners fall into the discount chain mentality and try to make price the feature.

A client we once worked with offers an entertainment/dining experience that is one of the most expensive in town. But they make it so unique that you just can't compare them to other restaurants. In the year we worked with them, they had 10,000 more guests than the prior year. And this is their twentieth year in business.

There seems to be a new iPod model every six months or so. And people keep buying them even as the price goes up. Why? Because they want the best and the newest. Not necessarily the cheapest.

You know you can get a decent MP3 player for around $80 from an electronics store? But they don't sell nearly as well as the iPod. Why? Because iPod is the best and everyone knows it (even if it's not really). Apple has created a unique experience that delivers a compelling and clear preference.

Success leaves clues. Are you looking for them?

Your Marketing Gravitational Positioning Statement

These days, we are all familiar with global positioning systems (GPS). A GPS in your car, on your watch, or in your hand can help you determine your location, speed, and direction—anywhere on the Earth. It's a pretty helpful tool and many people can't drive without one.

Now critical to navigation worldwide, GPS is a useful tool for commerce and science. It's important to know where you are and where you are going, wouldn't you agree?

Likewise, a marketing GPS (which stands for *Gravitational Positioning Statement*) can help any business owner or sales professional get a clear understanding of their position in the marketplace and where they are going. Perhaps more important, by understanding this yourself, you'll be able to communicate it with your prospects, which will make them more likely to want to interact with you.

A GPS is essentially a clear and simple statement that defines who you are, the primary benefits you offer, and what makes you different from those around you. It embodies your primary point of differentiation and should be easy to understand and easy to communicate.

Your GPS will become the core of all the marketing that you do; it will become your guiding light that provides a constant reference for what you're trying to accomplish and the benefits you are trying to communicate.

A powerful GPS will heighten your Gravitational Potential and cause more people to be attracted to you and your business, naturally. You'll be easy to find and easy to relate to. Your message will be clear and understandable. People will know why they want to do business with you and what they can expect.

Creating an effective GPS is the hard work that makes marketing and selling easy. Getting it right reduces the friction and resistance to the process and encourages the right people to come to you and the wrong people to go somewhere else.

Finding Your Emotional Benefits

On a clean sheet of paper or a spreadsheet, spend a few minutes listing the features of your core product or service (one product or service at a time).

Next to each feature, list a benefit that explains why the feature would be important to your customer. If a feature is not important, write "not important." You want to focus on the biggest benefit your customers can derive from each feature.

In the next column, list the value- or emotional-based desire (g-forces that your prospect has that are related to each benefit. It may not be as easy as it sounds. If a benefit doesn't have an attached emotional appeal, leave it blank.

Take a look at the worksheet you've been creating. Are any of the benefits or emotional appeals that you offer unique? Are there any that are so unique that your competitors don't offer them (or aren't talking about them)? Find them. *Highlight them.* Remember them.

Ask yourself, "Are the emotional appeals my product or service offers equal to the desires of my prospects?"

If the features of your product or service offers benefits that trigger emotions that people are actually *feeling*, then you can build a strong emotional link with your customers.

Circle the benefits that actually solve real problems or create real emotional benefits.

Are any of the benefits you circled the same as the unique benefits you highlighted a moment ago? You only need one match to make it big.

This is where the cream rises to the top. To truly win this game, you and your company must provide products or services with unique features to offer real emotional satisfaction.

If you have a product or service that delivers a big emotional benefit, but your competitors do too, what do you really have?

If you have a unique flair and features that your competitors do not have, but that aren't emotionally appealing to your customers, what do you really have?

To deliver a truly high ROI for your customers, your product or service must pack a wallop of a benefit and elicit some powerful emotions. Otherwise, your customers won't be into it. They won't pay attention, and they certainly won't pay money.

If you don't have any unique benefits with real emotional appeals, you may need to scrap the project.

But repeat the exercise to see if you can come up with anything. Try a new twist on an existing product or service that adds uniqueness and emotional appeal.

We believe it is possible for almost any company to find one of these. And one is all it takes.

Under your list of products and features on your worksheet, describe in sentence form the unique, emotionally charged, high-ROI benefits you can deliver. This is the beginning of your GPS.

Crafting a Gravitational Positioning Statement

Once you have identified that one unique, emotionally charged, high-ROI benefit you deliver, you can begin crafting a powerful statement that you'll be able to use as the backbone of all of your marketing efforts.

Begin by considering these elements:

- The statement must complete the following: "Buy this product, and you will get [this specific benefit]."
- The statement must be something that your competition does not offer.
- The statement must be strong enough to attract new customers.
- The statement must focus on what's in it for the customer. It shouldn't be focused on you or your company.

By keeping these four ideals in mind, you can quickly create a very compelling statement that makes a solid promise to your prospects.

Let's examine some excellent Gravitational Positioning statements:

- *Taco Bell:* "Get full with the Big Bell value menu."
- *Head & Shoulders:* "You get rid of dandruff."
- *Olay:* "You get younger-looking skin."
- *Red Bull:* "You get stimulation of body and mind."
- *Domino's Pizza:* "You get fresh, hot pizza delivered to your door in 30 minutes or less—or it's free."
- *FedEx:* "Your package absolutely, positively has to get there overnight."
- *M&M's:* "The milk chocolate melts in your mouth, not in your hand."
- *Wonder Bread:* "It helps build strong bones 12 ways."
- *Colgate:* "Cleans your breath while it cleans your teeth."
- *So Social:* "Give me $10 and I'll guarantee you a fun, business-generating networking event with absolutely no membership fees."

- *Unnamed Auto Dealership:* "You're approved, or I'll give you the car."
- *Joel Bauer's Trade Show Business:* "Crowds ... Guaranteed!"

This is what you want to develop for yourself.

Once you have your statement down, you're miles ahead of 99 percent of other businesses and sales professionals out there.

You can use your statement:

- As a headline in your advertising.
- As an introduction at networking events.
- On your business card.
- On direct mail letters.
- In every communication, you have with your prospects and customers.

 Bonus Resource

Jim and Travis' GPS Creator
This handy little spreadsheet will help you create a GPS that will have your prospects eating out of the palm of your hand. This a special gift from us to you. To get it visit www.GravityBook .com/bonus.

From the Trenches

We were at this highbrow networking event at a really posh private club in Orlando. There were a lot of people there.

They began the meeting and gave everyone a chance to stand up and share who they were and what they do. Hearing what these people had to say was almost comical.

(continued)

I think the worst one in the room had to be one real estate agent. There are plenty of agents and there are plenty of networking events, but that doesn't mean every agent doesn't have a chance. If you're good, you have an even greater chance because most are bad, and this one was the worst.

She stands up and says, "I'm a realtor. We buy, we sell, we're pretty much all the same. I spent a lot of money to print a brochure in color. I have them here if anyone wants one. Please come see me, I'm trying to get rid of them."

At the end, during the open networking, guess how many people went up to her and asked for the brochure. None. If she's not excited about what she does, she's definitely not going to get anybody else excited about it.

Her problem goes so far beyond networking. Someone might say she's just nervous talking in front of people. But I believe the real problem was that her message wasn't clear, or maybe she didn't have a message at all. She didn't know what she offered that was different, unique, or better than anyone else.

When you choose an agent, there are thousands to choose from. The same is true for most businesses. Why in the world would anybody choose you? That's what the GPS is about. It is the message that causes somebody to choose you. She had her opportunity and she blew it.

If she's running any advertising, then she's probably missing the opportunity there, too. She's probably sitting around scratching her head wondering why it isn't working.

Create Irresistible Attraction

Give Them What They Want so They Can't Say No . . .

In many science fiction movies when aliens visit Earth, they come in peace, sometimes bearing gifts. They're on to something that marketers can use to their benefit.

> The golden rule of intergalactic marketing is *give value first*.

Now armed with a tightly defined target and a powerful GPS, you're probably anxious to start screaming from rooftops and announcing your newfound marketing clarity to the world (or more specifically, to your target).

It might sound something like this:

"Hello, world! Listen to what I have to offer you! It's fantastic! And it can be yours for only $99.95!"

Pause. Before you ask a prospect to pay attention or money, you need to give them value first.

We completely understand the burning desire to spread your message to the world. It's about darned time you start making money with this deal. But we urge you to be patient just a little longer. At this phase, there are two problems for most business professionals.

Marketing Problem Number 1

Your GPS may be based on concrete emotional benefits. But your product or service may be complicated or costly.

If you need to speak with a prospect for more than about 15 seconds before they will buy, or if what you're selling costs more than about $30, you're going to need to take a few more steps before you start asking people to buy.

Namely, you'll need to create an intermediate step between stranger and customer, a step that people can easily understand and picture themselves taking. It's got to be low cost, no risk, and painless.

It should be a step they can take that will further cement the bond between you and them.

This method that we call *hook and permit* involves making the customer take two steps before they buy something. In the first step, they indicate that they're interested by requesting more information; in the second step, they make the purchase. You *hook* them with a promise of a big benefit, and they *permit* you to tell them more.

Marketing Problem Number 2

Even if you have wisely chosen a target and have developed a scorching hot GPS, if you jump out and start selling right away you'll be right back where you started.

People really don't want to be sold anything, but people really love to buy. There's an important distinction between the two. Being sold something suggests something has been done to you, whereas buying is something that you do yourself. You go from the object of an action, to the person taking the action.

The goal is to entice your prospects into choosing to buy. This must be done gently and carefully. It's a process of seduction.

Imagine yourself single, standing in a bar, scoping out the scene, looking for a mate. Now picture the perfect person right there before your eyes, sitting all alone. Seems intelligent, very attractive, and ready for the taking. What might you say?

Would you go right for the close and say, "Hi, would you like to go home with me?" Probably not. The answer to that question is most always no.

Instead, for the best result, you would probably ask something like, "Hi, may I buy you a drink?" Much better. And the answer to that question is frequently yes.

Then you buy the drink, you chat a bit, you find out if there's a possible emotional connection, if you have something to offer that the other person wants, and discuss moving forward or taking the next step—maybe dinner as an intermediate step.

Fortunately, for most, it's far easier to seduce a potential customer than it is to seduce a potential date.

Most people don't go right for the close when it comes to creating a personal relationship. But most business owners insist on going for the immediate close when it comes to generating business. Why?

Before we talk about the solution to this problem, let's talk for a moment about the *Mighty Wall of Mistrust*.

Mighty Wall of Mistrust

In any transaction that ever occurs—whether it's buying a car, buying a house, buying a pencil eraser, doing an oil change, hiring an accountant, hiring an attorney, choosing a hospital and a doctor to give birth to your first child—whenever there's a sale that's about to be made or an action that's about to be taken, there is a wall that exists between the buyer and the seller. In some situations, the wall is like a speed bump and in others it's more like the Great Wall of China.

Obviously, we would prefer if it was more like the first, rather than the latter, but sadly that is usually not the case. Regardless of size, that wall always exists. It's called the *Mighty Wall of Mistrust.*

This potent barrier is the roadblock for most business owners and salespeople. To some, it is an insurmountable obstacle that renders failure.

So what is this mighty wall and what determines its height?

The wall is made up of everything a prospect feels, thinks, does and doesn't know about you and your product or service. It is made up of preconceived notions, past experiences, prejudices, stereotypes, assumptions, bad and good information, research, hearsay, feelings, gut reactions, upbringing, and the like. It's made up of fear, anxiety, and doubt. All of this stuff builds a wall between the buyer and the seller. It is as powerful and solid as rock.

The buyer, at the beginning of the transaction, does not trust the seller. That's because profit motive, by definition, creates a possibility for the seller to take advantage of the buyer for profit. There's inherent risk involved in the transaction.

What it's really built of, the glue that holds it all together, is basically the worry or the doubt that the money traded for the product or service provided or rendered will be worth more than the value received.

So to make a transaction happen, you need to climb over that Mighty Wall of Mistrust. This happens when any sale is made. Different types of sales and the frequency of sales will set the wall at different heights. When you've done business with someone multiple times, the wall gets lower and lower. When the product price is very low, the wall is very low. But the higher the product price, the greater the wall. The newer the relationship, the greater the wall.

Every businessperson, every business owner, every entrepreneur, every salesperson, every marketing director deals with this every day, all day, whether they understand it or realize it or not. If you've ever made a sale, you've climbed over this wall or you've gotten the prospect to climb over the wall.

Most marketing and sales processes chip away at the wall. They take little chunks out of the wall, small pieces over a long period of time.

Gravitational Marketing will help you bulldoze the wall of mistrust more easily and more quickly. This accelerates the rate at which you can close the sale by causing the prospects to raise their hands and say, "I'm interested. . . . Sell to me!" Now you can divert your marketing and sales efforts, resources, and attention to those interested people to seduce them into a sale. The sooner the Mighty Wall of Mistrust falls, the shorter the sales cycle.

Bait

In *How to Win Friends and Influence People* (New York: Simon & Schuster, 1936, p. 42), Dale Carnegie related this story:

> *I often went fishing up in Maine during the summer. Personally, I am very fond of strawberries and cream, but I have found that for some strange reason, fish prefer worms. So when I went fishing, I didn't think about what I wanted. I thought about what they wanted. I didn't bait*

the hook with strawberries and cream. Rather, I dangled a worm or a grasshopper in front of the fish and said: 'Wouldn't you like to have that?'

Indeed. To attract customers, we've got to dangle something very attractive in front of them and ask them to come have a taste. But there's no need to over complicate this process. Fish like worms, and most people like free stuff. Offering something for free is often the cheapest and most effective bait you can use.

Yes, we're going to ask you to give something away for free.

This may seem counterintuitive at first. You may be thinking, "I need cash to flow *into* my business, not *out* of my business."

And you're right. But, if you want to get anything out of your customers, you're going to have to give them something first. Think about the free drink in the bar.

So what can you give for free? This is the best news you'll get all day. Information makes a wonderful piece of free bait. And information is very elastic, meaning it can be positioned as very valuable, perceived as very valuable, can actually be very valuable, but only costs you pennies. That makes free information our number one choice.

What makes this information so valuable is that it carries with it the promise of a solution. The information, when packaged properly, taps directly into those g-forces we talked about earlier. Think of this piece of free information, this piece of bait, as a widget. And any company can create free information widgets using their expertise.

For example, if you are a plumber who promises to keep homes leak free for life, you could create free information your prospects could use to prevent leaks from occurring in the first place or a homeowner's emergency leak survival kit in case the leak has already sprung.

If you're a financial planner who offers to help families plan for college tuition, you could offer free information that helps families get their ducks in a row so they can apply for grants, loans, or scholarships.

But you protest, "If I tell them how to do what I do, won't I work myself out of a job?"

No. People have an almost insatiable desire for answers and information, especially when information comes from an expert and promises a solution. But simultaneously, they are lazy and generally lack the competence required to do what you do.

The auto mechanic could send you the official mechanic's guide to fixing your car. But does that mean you will want to or be able to replace your water pump? For most people, the answer is no.

Ultimately, your free information should serve not only to educate, but also to prepare your prospects to do business with you and to motivate them to take the next step in the sales cycle.

So the mechanic would be well served to provide his prospects with information about how to avoid costly repairs. Does this mean he sits back like the Maytag man with no customers coming through the door?

No, because to avoid costly repairs, you must perform preventative maintenance. In fact, this mechanic could send information about how to change your oil properly and most people would look at the complicated instructions and say, "Uncle! It's just easier to pay a mechanic." And who will they choose? Of course, the expert who provided them with the free information in the first place—especially if that information comes along with a special offer.

Free Information You Can Create

Free information comes in many shapes and sizes. It can range from down and dirty, black and white, homegrown material that is very inexpensive to slick, glossy, fancy material, which can be very expensive. It can be something that's created in an hour, or it could take months. We've found that the cheaper and simpler material works just fine.

Free Reports, E-Books, White Papers, and How-To Guides

This sounds harder than it actually is. Write 5, 10, 15, or 20 pages that share the information in your brain with your prospects. If you're not confident in your writing skills, record it and hire a transcriptionist to type it. Or write an outline and hire a student or professional writer to expand on your outline.

Don't have anything to say? Do some quick research on the Internet and find articles that pertain to your offering and target. Contact the writer and ask if you can reprint the articles. Do a search for "free articles" and you will find several databases of articles that are all free for the taking with proper accreditation. String a few of these articles together as a helpful how-to guide for your prospects.

We highly recommend that you do the writing yourself because this will greatly assist you in positioning yourself as the expert.

If you can open your word processor and bang out a few pages, do it. It will be one of the most efficient investments of your time you have ever made.

When you've completed your written masterpiece, take it down to the office supply store or a printer and ask them to print it as a booklet on 11 × 17 inch paper and bind it with a saddle stitch (staple). Put a heavy, brightly colored cardstock cover on it, and voila, you have a little book (see Figure 7.1).

If you'd prefer to create an e-book, just have your document converted to a PDF. There are several PDF-maker programs available online for low cost.

The advantage to using an e-book format is cost. There basically is none. But a printed booklet generally carries far more impact and credibility. You'll have to weigh the pros and cons for your business. We highly recommend using printed material. We've seen as much as a 100 times greater response to printed material compared to the same information offered as an e-book.

When you create your free printed material, make sure that you combine the information with a persuasive message for taking the next step with your company. Whether it's ordering the product, arranging a sales presentation, having a face-to-face meeting or anything else, make sure to heavily promote that next step and clearly indicate the emotional benefits the prospect will experience as a result.

In the end, your masterpiece should be an information-rich sales letter.

Free Audio Programs

Can't type? Prospects can't read? Make an outline and record a 10-, 20-, or 30-minute audio program. If you contact a small, local radio station, you'll generally find they are willing to give you 30 minutes of

For high-end professional service firms and the hard-working sales-people within them:

"If you're tired of wasting tons of time and cash on marketing that doesn't work...if you're ready to stop cold-prospecting, become the expert, and start generating a steady stream of qualified prospects, review this innovative guide immediately."

THE TEN
TALL TALES
of Traditional Marketing
(that cost you tons)

REVEALED: The truth behind marketing lies that cost you millions in time, cash, and opportunity...lies that have been passed down by generations of marketing hacks, sales imposters and two-bit chiselers.

You'll get the TRUTH behind lies like these:

presented by:
Travis Miller & Jimmy Vee, Scend LLC
© 2004. All rights reserved.

> ➤ "It's all about getting your name out there..."
> ➤ **"You can't expect results over night..."**
> ➤ "You need to buy a bigger ad..."
> ➤ **"You should be cheaper than your competition..."**
> ➤ "You can't control word-of-mouth advertising..."
> ➤ **"You need to brand your business..."**
> ➤ "You need to make cold-calls..."

FIGURE 7.1 Free Report Cover. Information is a cheap and highly valuable widget to exchange for a prospect's permission. Here is the cover of one of our very first reports, *The Ten Tall Tales of Traditional Marketing*. Printed on yellow card stock, this art provided a cover to a 38-page free information widget that we used to attract customers through both manual and paid marketing efforts. Many business owners across the country in every imaginable business niche have since repurposed this cover.

studio time and edit your recording (to remove any mistakes and add some music to the front and back) for between $100 and $150. Not bad.

When your program is done, you can have it burned onto audio CDs for between $1 and $2 each with a color label.

Once again, make sure that you combine the information with a persuasive message for taking the next step with your company and clearly indicate the emotional benefits the prospect will experience as a result.

Checklists, Charts, and Worksheets

Some businesses can use these very effectively. Create a checklist that outlines the steps a prospect needs to take before they can attain the benefit promised by your GPS (e.g., precollege funding checklist or leak-free home checklist).

When you do ultimately meet with a prospect who has already completed a checklist or worksheet, the selling process will be much smoother because you can use their data to present to them.

These are excellent additions to an audio recording or a printed booklet.

Videos and DVDs

Do you have a product or service that can only be demonstrated visually (like photography or videography)? Consider creating a sample video or DVD that showcases your work and gives your prospects an opportunity to see what you do.

Just don't forget to make your pitch!

Recorded Messages

Free recorded messages, also known as hotlines, are a quick and easy way to deliver valuable and relevant information instantly and on demand. You can use a free recorded message just like a booklet. Outline the information you want to get across, write a script, and then read it.

There are a number of toll-free services you can use to get a toll-free number and put up a message.

If your industry has a less-than-honest reputation, create a consumer hotline that tells prospects the crucial information they need to know before making a buying decision to avoid being ripped off or scammed.

At the end of your message, offer the listener a next step, outline the benefits, and ask them to take action.

$ **Expert Resource**

Ron Romano is a master of turning prospects into profits. Ron says, "Do not spend another single penny on marketing and lead generation until you read my important information."

What information does Ron want you to know? You'll have to visit the resource site to find out but we'll give you a hint.

What Ron does for his customers is simply amazing. His company, Automated Marketing Solutions, helps business owners automate their lead attraction process through the use of hotlines, online lead capture sites, and other technology solutions.

Learn more about using these tools in your business by going to the Gravitational Marketing resource site at www.GravityBook.com/hotline.

Personal Widgets

Booklets, CDs, checklists, or videos just can't do justice to some products or services. In some cases, a personal, face-to-face meeting is what's required.

But presentations, pitches, demonstrations, and such are all sales terms and are unlikely to excite or motive your prospects.

Instead, create a personal widget such as a free audit, free inspection, free exam, free update, free evaluation, or free analysis. These names indicate that the meeting will hold some value and not just be a sales pitch.

Creative Names

Whatever kind of information you choose to use, be sure to name it something appealing that sounds valuable and enticing, like something other than a sales pitch.

Here are some excellent examples of free information with effective names that we've encountered or created:

- Free Night Time Renewal Kit.
- Complete Success Makeover Evaluation.
- 17 Ways to Qualify for Federal College Grant Money.
- Common Car Scams to Avoid.
- 101 Questions to Ask—Before You Hire a Plumber.
- How to Get $100,000 in Life Insurance Coverage for Just $5.
- What the Government Doesn't Want You to Know about the Local Water.
- Free Home Energy Inspection.
- Secrets of How to Buy the Home of Your Dreams—Even with Less than Perfect Credit.
- Free Property Value Analysis.
- Learn to Ride a Motorcycle—FREE.

One Critical Piece of Information

Regardless of what type of free information you decide to use, you'll need to be sure to include one critical item: a call to action.

Remember, one of the primary purposes of this free information is to motivate prospects to take the next step.

So before you develop your widget, you need to determine what that next step is.

Make consistent reference to that next step in your material, and constantly underscore the benefits that come from taking the step.

For example, throughout and at the end of your printed report, you might say, "To learn more about what I've discussed, call me at 555-555-5555 to schedule your free, no obligation personal analysis."

Measuring Marketing Effectiveness

On any journey, it's always wise to know how far you've gone and how far you have left to go. It's crucial to measure your progress along the way. Sadly, many business owners set out on the long marketing journey with no measuring devices and no way to quantify their results.

Most people wouldn't get in their car and drive 1,000 miles wearing a blindfold. But many business owners are all too anxious to spend money and time on marketing that they can't measure and results that they can't quantify. That's just as dangerous.

But how do you measure your marketing?

Bite the Brand That Feeds You

As a business owner or independent sales professional, we urge you to erase the word and concept of branding from your internal vocabulary. Almost all business advertising focuses on branding. And almost all business advertising fails.

What is brand advertising? Let's define it as any kind of advertising done with the sole purpose of:

- Getting your name out there.
- Increasing visibility.
- Boosting your image.
- Raising exposure.

These are the most common goals of brand advertising for any business. They are goals to be avoided.

A brand advertisement can be characterized by the following traits (not a complete list):

- No headline or a headline that is the name of the business.
- The term "one-stop shop" is used.
- Good service is mentioned.
- The number of years in business is talked about.
- The primary feature of the ad is the logo.

- Images in the ad don't add selling power.
- The ad tries to be cute, clever, or funny.
- There are no real benefits discussed.
- Features may be mentioned, but not explained.
- There's no clear contact information.
- There's no clear next step.

It's not uncommon to hear an advertiser say, "We're getting our name out there."

Nonsense. Coca-Cola is getting their name out there. You're counting grains of sand, and it won't get you anywhere.

Brand advertising feels good, boosts your ego, and wins awards. It's fun to show to people at church, but it doesn't earn you money. Brand advertising only achieves success by accident or by chance.

The worst part about brand advertising is that you never really know if it works. The only way to measure brand advertising is to measure this month's sales against last month's sales or to conduct a survey or focus group to determine how many people are aware of your business. But you can't deposit awareness in the bank.

If you're running more than one ad and sales are up, you have no idea which ad produced the results. So you keep running all the ads.

John Wannamaker once said, "Half of my advertising is wasted, I just don't know which half."

For a business owner or sales professional, wasting half of your ad budget generally means you need to stop advertising or go out of business. Both are bad options.

Response-Oriented Gravitational Marketing

In contrast, response-oriented Gravitational Marketing is the exact opposite of brand advertising.

With Gravitational Marketing, you intentionally design ads to get people to take specific actions. You back up your request with a promise of a big benefit. And you communicate that promise with compelling headlines and ad copy.

Typically, a response-oriented ad will feature a tracking mechanism that allows the advertiser to know with certainty which ads are working and which ads are not. That way, you can cancel the ads that fail.

Some typical characteristics of a Gravitational Marketing advertisements include:

- Prominent headline.
- Compelling ad copy.
- Benefit-driven message.
- Specific call to action (next step).
- A tracking mechanism for determining the ad's success (special code or discount).
- Pictures that make sense and are congruent with the message.
- A general lack of cuteness, cleverness, or humor.

What you need to be concerned with is abandoning the quest for cute, clever, or funny ads that strive to get your name out there. You need to begin requiring that all of your advertising delivers a measurable result.

The goals of a Gravitational Marketing advertisement are to get someone to:

- Pick up the phone.
- Visit a web site.
- Come to your store.
- Buy something.
- Take the next step.
- Request your free information.

Notice the conspicuous lack of anything brand, name, or image related in that list.

How to Track an Ad's Effectiveness

It really is quite simple, and yet most advertisers don't do it: Make a special and distinct offer in each ad. Ask prospects to dial a particular extension or call a specific phone number or visit a special web site or ask for a certain person. Using something that allows you to know where the lead came from is a good idea.

You might try asking prospects to:

- Call 1-800-999-9999 and dial extension 215.
- Send in this coupon (which contains a tracking code).
- Call now and ask for Susan.
- Mention this ad and receive (special offer not mentioned anywhere else).

Doing this allows you to associate a lead source with every single lead. When you run an ad, you can go back at the end of the month and count up how many leads the ad delivered. After a while, you can find out how many sales were generated from a specific ad. This kind of data is what allows you to determine whether an ad is working or not.

Branding as a Side Effect: Brandscending

"But what about our name? I'm spending all this money. I want people to know who we are and think of us when they need our services."

First of all, forget it. If you spend money trying to accomplish that, you're out. But that's not to say that it won't happen on its own.

You can only focus on one thing in your advertising at a time. You can (1) focus on branding and leave the hope that someone might buy something or contact you to chance, or (2) you can focus on getting people to buy something and leave the hope that your company's name gets out there to chance.

Option (2) is the better choice.

As you advertise consistently, your name will get out there whether you want it to or not. How much that helps is another story. But it does happen.

Branding occurs as a side effect of consistent Gravitational Marketing. But sales rarely happen as a side effect of brand advertising.

Your First Gravitational-Style Advertising Campaign

Now that you understand and buy into the concept of marketing only for direct results and not for some elusive form of brand awareness; you can feel confident going forward into the world of paid advertising.

Paid advertising, when done correctly, is the most immediate and efficient form of marketing. Rather than cold calling, networking, knocking on doors, or some other form of barbaric sales bull-work—which all require you to trade in your time and sanity and only allow you to speak to one person at a time—you can advertise wisely and speak to hundreds, thousands, or even millions at once.

As a business owner, it's easy to feel like your money is more valuable than your time, especially if you have no money, no clients, and lots of time.

But relying only on time-exchange-based marketing, like cold calling or networking, means you'll have to wait a long time to actually experience results.

Even when you're starting out, you must treat your time as the most valuable asset you have. Guard it with your life. The unique qualities you have are important and valuable, and you must spend the maximum percentage of your time on those things that you are uniquely qualified to do. Everything else you pay someone else to do.

Unless you are a superstar cold prospector and love cold calling or networking or any other form of burning shoe leather, you should avoid it.

Instead, use your time to learn about and plan effective marketing techniques that properly leverage your investment. Paid advertising is one such technique.

It's Simpler than You Think

Advertising effectively is not nearly as difficult or complicated as it seems to be. It's far simpler than the agencies want you to think it is, and it's much clearer and easier to understand than most marketing books (especially the voodoo books about branding) would have you believe.

In fact, when starting out, you can advertise like a pro after learning only one simple technique. It's the hook and permit technique we mentioned earlier.

The concept is this: Don't ask your advertisement to carry the entire burden of making the sale on its shoulders. Instead, break the prospecting and selling process up into pieces, and assign only some of the pieces to your ads.

For instance, don't require a single ad to Gravitate, Captivate, Invigorate, and Motivate. It would be a dream if you could place a small ad and then watch the orders roll in. It's possible in some cases, but if your sale is complicated or costly, this scenario is unlikely.

Instead, we ask our ads to merely capture attention, generate some interest, and volley that interest into the next, small, intermediate step—like the free information we just talked about. We ask our ads to Gravitate.

Let's examine the ad copy from a good, benefit-driven, response-oriented advertisement that *does not* follow this approach:

Make Your Dog's Year and Make Up for All Those Missed Walks and Long Stays in the Crate! Get a keepsake video of your precious pooch starring in his or her own feature film. Fido can be in an old western, a murder mystery, an action drama, or even a love story! Your custom video shoot is only $299. But mention this ad and receive five minutes of extra custom video. Call today! 555-555-5555.

Now, let's review ad copy for the same offering, but this time by using the Hook and Permit technique:

Make Your Dog's Year and Make Up for All Those Missed Walks and Long Stays in the Crate! Get a keepsake video of your precious pooch starring in his or her own feature film. Fido can be in an old western, a murder mystery, an action drama, or even a love story! See a sample video and receive a FREE copy of "7 Ways to Pamper Your Pet for under $7." Sent by mail. No obligation. Call today! 555-555-5555 or visit www.poochparty.com/video.

Do you recognize the difference? Of course, the second ad doesn't ask for the sale. It asks for an intermediate step.

As it turns out, $299 is a lot of money for someone to decide to spend on the spot by looking at a small ad. Most people are going to require some additional information before committing. You would, wouldn't you?

But since the first ad pushes the sale, the average person is going to be hesitant to call because she'll be worried that the sales pitch will continue on the phone. Without more information about the product, the reader may disqualify herself by deciding that $299 is too much to pay. Without seeing the finished product, it's likely someone may think that.

The second ad doesn't mention a price for the video. Instead, it offers a sample video and a great little premium for requesting the video (like a legal bribe).

If you ran these two ads back to back, one month after another, you would receive many more calls from the second ad than from the first ad.

What has happened in this scenario is that an interested prospect has identified herself to you. A person who requests your package has said, "I am interested in making my dog happy, and I might like to see my dog in a video. Tell me more."

That's what we're aiming for here: "Tell me more." Essentially, you're getting permission to sell to this person.

Your budget will most likely restrict you from marketing to the entire universe, but a hook and permit approach allows you to run small ads, asking people to take small steps. Then, you can unleash the full fury of your marketing campaign on only those people who identify themselves as interested, thereby making your marketing budget go further.

From the Trenches

I was watching *Seinfeld* reruns last night and saw a really great ad that I had to share with you.

The ad was for Match.com. Match.com is an online dating service whose major competitor is eHarmony.com. EHarmony. com runs tons of offline and online advertising but up until last night I had not seen any offline advertising for Match.com.

Let me tell you why this ad was so great. The entire commercial was for one thing: a free guide that you could request by calling a toll-free phone number or by going to their web site.

The title of the guide itself was great marketing worth studying. The guide was called, "How to Find the Right Person in 90 Days: A Step-by-Step Guide Based on Millions of Relationships Inspired by Match.com."

The ad was effective because of its clarity. They didn't junk it up by trying to sell the service and the guide in the same ad. They only focused on selling the guide. What they were actually selling was a next step in the marketing process.

Once someone requests the guide, Match.com knows they have an interested prospect, and then they spend their time and dollars marketing to that prospect.

PART

Gravitational Marketing Attraction Techniques

8

Activate Your Gravitational Attraction

Now we're going to discuss the Gravitational Attraction Techniques that we have found to be most effective. Some of these techniques involve paid advertising, and others involve manual labor or free publicity. All of these techniques require you to expend either money or time. When implemented, each of these will attract prospects and customers to your business right away.

It's about getting people to raise their hands and identify themselves to you as interested in the solution or the benefits that you provide. Without knowing who they are, you have to talk to everybody. But by causing people to let you know who they are, how you can reach them, and that they're interested in learning more, you can focus your sales effort, energy, and marketing on these prospects specifically.

This will make your sales job significantly easier and less costly. Your life will become more enjoyable, simple, and prosperous because you know exactly who to spend your time, energy, and money focusing on.

Structuring Your Attraction Plan

The whole process starts with attracting a lead. To have a solid foundation to continue to build your business on, you need to use multiple attraction techniques simultaneously. Each Gravitational Attraction Technique you successfully implement ultimately becomes known as a lead source.

We typically recommend no less than five profitable lead sources, and those five should not all be from the same media. This means one lead source may be direct mail, one may be pay-per-click advertising, one may be a print magazine, one may be telemarketing, and one may be networking.

It's very dangerous to get all your leads from only one source. It makes your business very vulnerable.

If your entire business relies on only one lead source, what happens if you lose the opportunity to use that technique? If you rely on one magazine, what happens if that magazine goes out of business, its subscription rates unexpectedly go up, or the response rate goes down? If you rely only on direct mail, what happens as postage continues to rise or the post office decides it will no longer deliver the type of mail you send.

In an investment portfolio, experts say you should diversify by owning an array of stocks, funds, bonds, and other investments. You never want to have all your eggs in one basket. Similarly, you have to diversify your lead attraction portfolio.

What we've created for you here is a laundry list of many different lead attraction methods that you can pick and chose from based on what you think might be right for your business or your prospects and what fits your budget.

Gravitational Marketing Funnel

Imagine your business as a big building where the only way in and out is through one single, very narrow door. That's your one lead generation strategy in and out of the building. It's a bottleneck and gets clogged up very fast. If something happens to that door, everyone's either stuck outside or stuck inside. That's not a good thing. So we want to make sure you have multiple doors into your business. You do this with multiple effective lead attraction techniques.

Picture all of your lead sources dumping into a funnel. If you have five different lead sources and each one generates a number of leads each month or each week, they all end up in this funnel. What's important is what happens in that funnel. You want the process that is applied to all of those leads, no matter where they came from, to be the same.

Leads you attract online should receive the same follow-up as leads you attract in print, which should receive the same follow-up as leads you attract with direct mail. When you measure, you will be able to see the pattern of response that occurs from different lead sources, but if you follow up with them all differently, then you'll never know if one lead source is better than the other or if one follow-up method is better than the other.

Leads come into the funnel through all of the different lead sources that are created by implementing different Gravitational Attraction Techniques. No matter what source the lead comes from, they request your free widget. That's the entry point into your Gravitational Marketing funnel (Figure 8.1).

All of the leads who've raised their hands and requested the free widget become your prospects and move through the funnel. Our focus here is on filling your funnel with leads in the first place.

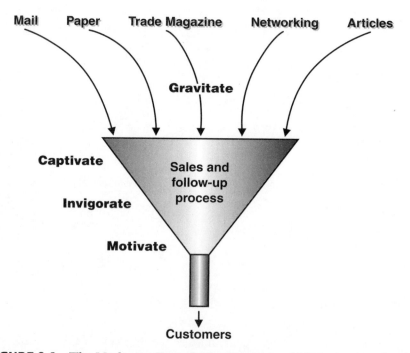

FIGURE 8.1   The Marketing Funnel. The Gravitational Marketing funnel is the lead attraction road map. Draw this funnel for your business, fill in your lead sources at the top, and outline your sales process to see what happens to a lead after it enters the funnel. This is your Gravitational Marketing plan and is missed by most business owners and entrepreneurs. The more lead sources you have pouring into your funnel, the more deal flow you will have. The more deal flow you have, the more selective you can become about who you work with. This makes your life more Enjoyable, Simple, and Prosperous (ESP).

Measuring Your Results

Generally, smaller businesses should start with the least expensive options and move toward the more expensive. But, keep in mind that less expensive isn't necessarily better than more expensive. The key metric to focus on is what we call *cost per lead*. It's the cost of an advertisement divided by the number of leads it generates. For example, if you spend $1,000 and generate one hundred leads, your cost per lead was $10.

The cost per lead of a very inexpensive technique, like a $20 networking event where you only get one good lead, is $20. Compare that to a lead generating method that's more expensive such as $5,000 spent on a full-page ad in your newspaper, which generates five hundred leads. That would be a $10 cost per lead. Can you see how the cost per lead was better on the more expensive media? You can't necessarily judge media by its cost, but instead by the results that it delivers.

Another metric that you want to consider is the ROI that's generated from those leads. You might find that one lead source produces a lower cost per lead, but the profit, the ROI from those leads, is not as high as leads from another source with a higher cost per lead.

To have any chance of measuring the cost per lead and the return on investment, you are going to have to know where every single lead comes from, keep a record of that information, and refer to it on a regular basis.

We recommend summarizing all of your leads attracted each month and categorizing them by lead source. Then note the cost to acquire those leads and the number of leads who turned into customers along with the amount of money they spent with you.

Armed with this data you'll be able to calculate the necessary measurements.

Bonus Resource

Jim and Travis' Lead Tracking Worksheet
This interactive spreadsheet will allow you to make the complicated tracking process easier. Type in your numbers and the

(continued)

spreadsheet will crunch your numbers and give you the data you need to be a marketing master.

You'll track measurements like cost per lead, value of customer, and ROI of a campaign. This special gift can be found at www.GravityBook.com/bonus.

Just because some lead sources are less profitable than others doesn't mean you should stop using them. We believe there are thin deals and thick deals and that it takes both kinds to be successful. Some lead sources yield more profit than others, but it's a combination of multiple lead sources that builds a business that's ESP.

Frequently, you'll find that the most profitable lead sources are the most limited. You just can't get as many leads from that source as you want. So you have to supplement with leads from other sources that may be more abundant but less profitable.

Conducting multiple transactions with the same customers again and again creates a profitable business. Frequently it makes sense to break even on the first transaction you have with a prospect just to acquire them as a customer. Some businesses even choose to lose money to acquire a new customer because they know what a customer is worth in the long term and are willing to invest money up front to make money in the future.

The bottom line is that you're going to need a cross section of some less expensive lead sources (based on cost per lead) that are really profitable and some more expensive lead sources (based on cost per lead) that may not be as profitable but that still make you money. You're going to need a mix. Stay diversified.

Ego versus Effectiveness

The more ego driven your marketing is, the less effective it is going to be. By ego driven, we mean that the marketing talks about your brand, it is corporate and stuffy, and it focuses solely on your company rather than on the benefits your prospects desire—it's more about you and less about them. Additionally, the more your marketing focuses on getting your name out there and the less it focuses on getting free widget requests, the less effective it's going to be.

But marketing that is focused on the prospect or the customer and their pains and desires and offers a clear next step (ideally requesting your free offer) has a far greater chance of being effective.

Imagine a seesaw with ego on one side and effectiveness on the other (Figure 8.2). The higher you want the effectiveness to be, the lower the ego side will have to go. The higher the ego side is raised, the lower the effectiveness will be.

If you get caught up in making fancy, glossy, professional looking marketing that doesn't pull the heartstrings of your prospects, then be prepared for the effectiveness to go down. The only people who will care about that marketing piece are you and your graphic designer.

If you relinquish your desire to build your brand and get your name out there and are willing to focus on solving the problems your prospects are dealing with, you'll end up with marketing that won't get you much attention at the country club but will cause prospects to gravitate to you. Ego in marketing is an ugly problem few business owners can afford.

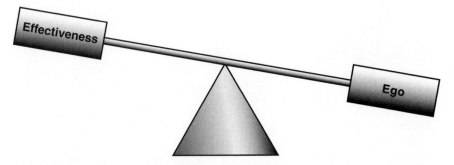

FIGURE 8.2 **Ego versus Effectiveness Scale.** This illustration demonstrates how ego in a marketing campaign and the effectiveness of that marketing campaign are counterbalanced. The more or less ego you put into your marketing campaign directly impacts how profitable it is. As simple as this may seem, many entrepreneurs and business owners still opt for more ego and then complain about the lackluster results of their campaigns. Don't be one of those people.

Next Step

Once you've clearly defined your market and your benefit-driven message, it's time to begin selecting the media and techniques you'll use to attract leads.

In the following chapters, we offer 36 unique Gravitational Attraction Techniques.

Some cost more money and some cost more time. This is the way it is with all lead attraction methods. There's always going to be a trade off. It's either going to cost you money or it's going to cost you time.

The more something costs, typically, the less time it will take. The less something costs, the more time it will take. Picture it as a scale of time and money and usually the more money that an advertising media costs, the less time it takes to actually be involved in it (Figure 8.3).

FIGURE 8.3   Time versus Cost Scale. The Time versus Cost scale affects many business owners' decisions about how to spend their marketing dollars. Your time (or lack thereof) is directly tied to the cost of a marketing method. Although more manual methods cost a great deal in time, mass media methods cost more money but work more automatically for you. Keep in mind the value of your time. Many business owners and entrepreneurs shortchange themselves and their business growth by opting to spend less money and more time, thinking it will make them more profitable. In reality, it costs them more in lost time and opportunity.

The more money you spend, the more automatic lead attraction becomes. The less money you spend, the more manual the lead attraction effort is.

The ultimate goal is to spend less of your time manually attracting leads by automating the process so that you can spend more time working with your customers and doing the things you love to do with you family and friends.

Attraction through Personal Effort

Technique 1: Networking

The important thing to keep in mind about networking is that it's basically no to low cost. It's one of the cheapest things that you can do to generate leads, but it's also almost always used improperly. Sure, you might have to pay for lunch, but you're usually paying for lunch anyway. You may have to pay $5 or $10 for an evening event, but compared to advertising that's a drop in the bucket.

Typically, networking takes time and costs little money. Depending on whether you place a higher value on your time or your money, networking may or may not be right for you.

Now, here's the mistake that most people make with networking events. You pay for a networking event. You go there. They usually have food; maybe they have a speaker; they do an icebreaker. You're there; you're involved in this icebreaker; maybe they give you a small window of time at the beginning to mingle and network and introduce yourself. But what happens is that you just end up being there instead of working the networking event.

Most people show up at a networking event believing that they're getting their name out there and they're increasing their visibility by being seen in the community. They believe this alone will attract business. But attracting business is a process. It doesn't happen on its own.

It's almost a mindset change. Most people attend these networking events and they see them as a social event to fraternize and meet with friends. Really, it's something that should be worked as a business opportunity. It's called networking for a reason. It's not called net socializing, net lunching, or net eating. It's networking.

Our Personal Networking Method, Part One

When we first started out, we basically had no money and we needed to meet people quickly. We had just about enough money to go to one networking event. We needed that one networking event to work or else we would have been in big trouble.

We knew that we had to stand out. We knew that we had to be recognized, and we knew that we could not be forgotten. We had to make a tremendous impact at this single event. We needed to be highly visible because what we noticed by going to networking events when we had jobs was that they were boring and everything was ordinary. Everything was blah and people were just lackadaisical and hanging around. We wanted to go in there and make an explosion.

We had already created a free information widget. In this case, it was a report called *The Ten Tall Tales of Traditional Marketing* (which is still available for free at www.GravitationalMarketing.com), and it told business owners and salespeople the problems that they had with their marketing and explained that we could fix them. So we went down to the office store and bought a label maker, and then we went to a company that made custom name tags and custom engraved items. We had them create plastic name tags and had them engraved with the phrase, "Ask me how I defy gravity." We left a blank space to put in the person's name.

We went to a networking event. One of us had a satchel filled with name tags, and the other had the label maker. We would walk up to people who were wearing handwritten paper name tags, and we would say, "I see you're wearing a paper name tag. Would you like me to make a nice, professional, permanent name badge for you? What's your name?" We would type the name into the label maker, print it out, pull the backing off the label, and slap it on one of our new name tags. Then we would pin it to the person's shirt (see Figure 9.1).

Now they had a professional hard plastic name badge that they could use during networking events, but it read, "Ask me how I defy gravity" on the bottom. So of course, they would ask, "What do I say if somebody asks me this question?" Everyone would ask that.

We said, "Well, I'll tell you how you can answer that question. We've written a free report, *The Ten Tall Tales of Traditional Marketing* that tells you exactly how you can defy gravity. By defying gravity, we mean that you can break the traditional binds that hold you down from growing in your business, and you can cause people to gravitate to you, instead of you having to go out and chase them." And they'd say, "Oh, that sounds really good." And we would say, "We can send it to you for free if you like." They'd hand us their

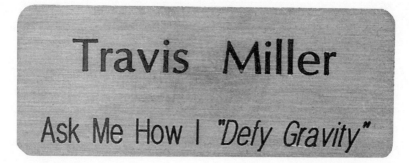

FIGURE 9.1 **Name Badge.** Our first big attraction stunt at networking events was making name tags for the event attendees. This is one of the name tags we used. Our tag line was engraved at the bottom of every name tag. This got people asking us how they should respond if asked, "How do I defy gravity?" Explaining this allowed us to get their permission to deliver our free information to them. It was also a very viral campaign. People would be lining up for a name tag and waiting to talk to us. Our goal ... make them come to us.

business card, and we would ask them for permission to send them the report.

Then we would put them on a list and send them the report, and we communicated with them via e-mail every 10 days. We're still communicating with those same people that we met at that first networking event years ago.

Back at our office, we put the contact information into a system that will automatically stay in touch with them for as long as we like. It's simple. Any kind of customer relationship management (CRM) database or autoresponder system will do this for you. Our plan was to go in there, give away the name tags, and create value first. We'd make friends, be unforgettable, and ask for their permission to send them information. Instead of just socializing, we were there getting permission to add people to our contact database.

We knew when we would go to an event how many name tags we started out with, and we would be able to count how many name tags we gave away. That gave us a metric, an ability to measure our performance for that networking event. When most people would go in and meet two, three, four, maybe five people at a networking event, we left having made name tags for 60 people and adding that many people to our database.

| $ | **Expert Resource** |

Clate Mask loves to turn small businesses into big businesses. Ever since he was a kid, he felt a nagging annoyance when someone referred to one of his ventures as a "small business." And his company Infusion Software has created the most powerful marketing CRM available today. If you want to go pro in marketing, you can't do it without Infusion.

We were skeptical about jumping from one marketing database to Infusion, but once we realized the power of Infusion, we've never looked back, and we recommend it to everyone. It's a critical resource that our companies depend on. You can learn more about automating your marketing by visiting the Gravitational Marketing resource site at www.GravityBook.com/automate.

Our Personal Networking Method, Part Two

After doing this at many networking events, we had made name tags for just about everyone we had met, so we needed something new. We needed another gimmick. We wanted a gimmick that was even more visible.

We went down to the mall and walked up and down the aisles. We were looking for something that was orange. We wanted some sort of orange apparel that would cause us to be very visible to the people at the networking event. We thought orange would be the most visible color. We looked at orange shoes. We looked at orange ties. We looked at orange suspenders. We looked at everything orange we could find, and what we finally settled on, as silly as it sounds, were orange visors. Then we had them embroidered. One read "defy" and the other read "gravity." This became our company slogan (see Figure 9.2).

We would put on these defy gravity visors and we'd go to the networking events and everybody would notice us. This goes back to

FIGURE 9.2 **Jim and Travis in visors.** Travis and Jim in their infamous orange visors. We became known for wearing these everywhere we went. We became local celebrities, and the visors attracted interested people and compelled them to ask us what we did for a living. Then we would use the *Hook and Permit* technique to capture their contact information and begin a relationship.

the rule of thirds. Immediately, one-third of the room said, "I gotta talk to those guys." Another one-third of the room said, "Those guys are jackasses!" And the other one-third was just too busy eating and drinking. But what happened is that one-third of the room, no matter where we went, would automatically gravitate to us and ask, "What do you guys do?"

Now that is the big question. That's the question you want people to come up to you and ask. Most of the time you're going around trying to tell people what you do, but we actually stood in one position at a networking event right by food and had a line of people waiting to talk to us. That's what you want to create.

Here's a quick tip for networking: stand near the food or near the bathroom because that's where everybody is going.

To prepare for when people would ask us what we do, we were constantly refining our GPS. In the beginning, it had to do with how to leverage the power of word-of-mouth marketing to cause people to come to you without actually spending any money. That seemed to be what people wanted to hear and what people wanted to talk about at that time. Because of the books that were popular at that time, this was a very popular concept. So we tapped into it. Before we went to every networking event, we would come up with a new way to spin that idea and that message into a new GPS. We would rewrite it and rehearse it sitting in the car in the parking lot before the networking event began.

It was almost like we had a show. We didn't go in there just planning to wing it. We had a prepared show. So when somebody asked us, it was like we were on Broadway. The show lights came on, we did the show, and then we did the same show over and over and over again for every single person who asked the question.

In our conversations, we would tell them what we did, then the other person would tell us what they did. It would always culminate in us asking them if they would like to receive our free report. We ended up writing a couple of other reports, *The Six and a Half Secrets of Successful Advertising* was one, *The Seven B's in Sensational* was another. We traded them out to see which one got the better reaction at the events and they all typically did pretty well.

The Proper Use of Business Cards

It's important to discuss the use of your business card at a networking event or in your day-to-day life. Most people try to give away their business cards at an event or at any time. Obviously, they hope it will cause somebody to call them and want to do business.

We decided we didn't want to give away business cards because we knew where they ended up—in the trash. We decided not to give away cards but rather to try to collect cards and garner permission at the same time. So we went around getting people's business cards, doing the show and asking them for permission to send them the report. We took their card and used that card to put their contact information into our database back at the office.

If you do give away a business card, there is a special kind of card you should give away. The cards we use always have an offer—for the free report, or for a free consultation, or something else for free. When we gave that card to people, it wasn't a typical worthless business card. (See Figures 9.3 through 9.5.) This card had value because we were making a substantial offer for them to get something at no risk and no cost from us. It was an offer. It might as well have been a gift card that we were giving out. People like gift cards. They don't generally care about business cards.

Jim and Travis Recommend

We've found the best printers on the planet!

Visit www.JimandTravisRecommend.com to find out who they are and how you can reach them.

Instant Celebrity

We started haunting the same networking events in different parts of town, and we became instantly recognizable and achieved a local celebrity status. We immediately energized any group when we showed up. We were built-in entertainment. Now, you may be thinking, "I'm not entertaining. I can't do that." You may be thinking that this is beneath you. But let us tell you what's beneath you. What is beneath you is running a business that makes no money. You deserve better than that. If that means you have to go out and put on an orange visor, then that's what we suggest you do.

A lot of people would say it's unprofessional. We say that someone who helps people achieve their goals is a professional. We say the guy who runs around in a visor and helps a lot of people is more professional

Are you making any of these **5 BUSINESS KILLING MISTAKES?**

With your **FREE, no-obligation** copy of "5 Business Killing Mistakes," you will learn how you may be able to:

- ☑ Make your partnership work and avoid a costly "business divorce."
- ☑ Make sure customers can and will pay you.
- ☑ Use this low cost way to protect your most valuable business asset.
- ☑ Keep your employees from putting you out of business.
- ☑ Prevent unnecessary competition.

5 BUSINESS KILLING MISTAKES

This **free, no-obligation report** gives you important information you may be able to use to increase your chances of success and to protect your investment.

Get your FREE copy now.

Visit www.OrlandoBusinessLawyer.com
or call (407) 649-7777

Attorney Ed Alexander, Office: Orlando. The hiring of a lawyer is an important decision that should not be based solely on advertising. Before you decide to hire a lawyer, ask us to send you free written information about our qualifications and experience.

FIGURE 9.3 **Ed Alexander Business Card.** (Top: Front) The front side of a great lead attraction business card. The salesperson in print does the work for you. This card is reprinted here with permission from Ed Alexander of OrlandoBusinessLawyer.com. (Bottom: Back) You can see how this card's primary purpose is to entice the prospect to take the next step by requesting his free report. This prescreens the prospects, qualifies and disqualifies them so Ed only has to spend his time with interested prospects who are predisposed to do business with him. This makes his sales process easier, less time consuming, and more profitable.

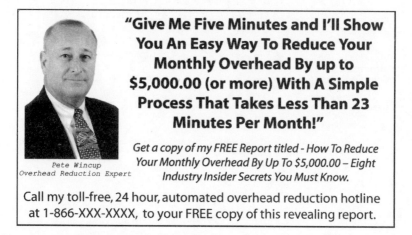

FIGURE 9.4 **Pete Wincup Business Card.** A lead attraction card designed by us for a client. Notice the big, bold benefit-driven headline and subheadline that offers a free report. Also notice that the name of the report makes it very desirable. The special toll-free number is able to track where the leads come from so that the client knows where his time and money are best spent reducing marketing waste and increasing profits.

than the guy who doesn't run around in a visor and doesn't help anyone because he can't get anyone to interact with his business.

Going back to the rule of thirds conversation, you do have to be prepared to take a little heat on this because you're going to turn some people off. But it's better than being ignored by everybody. We did create a buzz when we showed up at events, and if we weren't wearing the visors everyone would be asking, "Where are the visors?"

One time we actually got thrown out of a networking event at a fancy restaurant when the proprietor told us that we couldn't wear the visors indoors. We refused to take them off. So he had us escorted out.

At the next networking event, we got a little gun shy. It was at another fancy restaurant, so we didn't wear the visors. We got hammered by everyone at the networking event about why we weren't wearing the visors. We had to go back out to the car and get them.

That is the power of networking if done effectively. You want to stand out, be noticed, and be unforgettable somehow. And you want to

Give Me 5 Minutes And I'll Show You A Simple Way To Get Leads And Prospects To Call You, Pay More For Your Product Or Service And Beg You To Do Business With Them... Absolutely FREE!

Like it says on the front, I'm direct. So let's get right to the point. If you don't have a dependable and automatic system in place to generate leads and convert those leads into closed deals, you are missing out on a huge opportunity.

Listen, I may be the "Big Idea Man" but it doesn't take a rocket-scientist to know that more leads and more deals equal more money. But most of the people I talk to are sucking wind and struggling to truly enjoy life.

Jim and I have spent over 96 million dollars in advertising on every type of media imaginable. We've seen it all and done it all. But spending money without return is called "waste." And that doesn't work for me.

Here's what's important for you to know. For the $96 million spent we generated over $10 billion in revenue for our clients. That's a HUGE return on investment. Every dollar you spend in marketing should have a direct ROI and if it doesn't you're flushing your time and money right down the toilet.

Finally! Your Biggest Mystery—Solved...

For some reason unknown to me the art of simply & easily attracting customers seems to be a big mystery. There's plenty of senseless information and theory about brand building and differentiation, but when you get right down to it what you need is more deals—fast. That's what I'm obsessed about...creating ways and reasons for people to flock to you, cash in hand!

I'm Here To Help You & I'll Do It For Free!

Jim and I are serial entrepreneurs and we own several mult-imillion dollar businesses. We spend most of our time working on those businesses and writing, speaking and consulting with business owners and entrepreneurs all across the world. My time is limited but I'm willing to help you if you agree to take action.

Naturally Attract More Quality Customers Who Pay, Stay And Refer—Guaranteed!

So, Here's The Deal...

I want to help you make more money, live life on your own terms without compromise and put a tourniquet on the marketing waste that's bleeding you dry all while transforming your business and your life into something E.S.P.—that's Enjoyable, Simple and Prosperous. And I'm going to give you the opportunity on a silver platter, absolutely free! Exciting, huh? It should be.

Just go to: www.GravitationalMarketing.com. There is a ton of free resources you can get your hands on. And there's even an opportunity for you to get my Ultimate Free Gift Offer. Over $539.00 worth of free gifts and tools sent right to your door. All at no cost and no obligation.

So are you going to seize this truly amazing opportunity and take the action that could very well make all the difference for you? Gosh, I really hope so.

Sincerely Yours,

Travis Miller

The BIG Idea Guy

P.S. I don't believe in chance. I believe our paths have crossed for a reason. I'm glad I had a chance to meet you and hope we can create a prosperous relationship in the weeks, months and years to come.

Hey! Don't miss your chance to get free tools and gifts from our web site...

Free Tools & Gifts At www.GravitationalMarketing.com

FIGURE 9.5 Jim and Travis Business Card. The inside of our personal lead attraction business card. This one written in Travis' voice is full of powerful sales copy urging the reader to request our free information widget. This is a fold-over card and measures $3\frac{1}{2}$ inches wide by 7 inches tall when opened. This is similar to the vertical half page ad we recommend when buying print advertising.

capture people's contact information and stay in touch with them by adding them to your list of people that you communicate with on an ongoing basis.

If all of this isn't natural for you, then you can make it a game or a contest for yourself. Attend one networking event and collect a certain number of people's contact information, and then make a challenge to beat yourself the next time you go out. If you're constantly one-upping yourself, then you're just adding more and more contacts to your database.

The amazing thing is that by doing this over the course of a few months you can build a huge list. In those first six months that we networked, we created a database of thousands of people who we added to our newsletter and e-mail lists. We stayed in touch with all of them, converting more and more of them from strangers into friends. They were businesspeople and all of them were our potential clients.

Some of the people who received our free material would contact us, and then we would further those relationships by having meetings with them, eventually converting them into clients or referral partners.

Technique 2: Start a Networking Group

Starting a networking group is for the networking superstar who realizes that he doesn't like being at the mercy of the other networking groups. Once you've created your own list of people that you're talking to, your fan base, and once you are known as a connector, you can start your own networking group.

You can do this because as you meet all these people; you start to build your ability to connect certain people with other people. When you become good at that and you become confident with your ability to speak to other people, you can set up your own networking group where you are the leader. This can help you position yourself as an expert and cause people to come to you over your competitors.

Make the purpose of your networking group to connect people, generate leads, and share referrals. By being at the center of the group, you will naturally receive more referrals than others because you will be in the forefront of people's minds. You could even use the information from this book to help educate your members on the power of effective marketing.

That's the power of it right there. When you have a fan base, which is the hardest thing to achieve, you can create your own group positioning yourself as the head of that group. When you have the power of that fan base at your control, you can do many things. When you're the head of a networking group, you have a larger Gravitational Potential.

Bonus Resource

Jim and Travis' Networking Leaders Guide

This one-sheet guide will give you a basic formula for running an effective and fun networking event. You'll learn the basic structure and find articles about how to get more people to show up and refer others—just a little gift from your friends Jim and Travis.

Get it now at www.GravityBook.com/bonus.

You may still be wondering exactly how you can start your own networking group. First of all, it's very simple. You come up with a name. You should probably involve your company name or your personal name in the name of the group. You also need to find a location. You could go to a local coffee house or a local breakfast restaurant, ask for the manager and say, "I'd like to use the side room to host a networking event. The people I bring will come for breakfast, and they will buy breakfast or coffee and tip the servers well, and you will charge me nothing to have my meeting here." Most restaurant managers will agree with that. If the one you talk to doesn't, go to the next restaurant.

Then you take the list of people you've developed from networking over the past couple of months that you send e-mail or your newsletter to and you announce the start of your new group to all of them. Invite them to the new networking group and because they have had so much fun with you at the other networking groups, they'll figure it will probably be more fun than any others.

Because you've met these people at networking events already, you know they are interested in networking. So they're very likely to attend. Plan an activity, give everyone the chance to introduce himself or herself, speak a bit about your company, and offer everyone some free information, then let everyone network and make connections themselves.

There are a couple of key elements to hosting an effective networking group that people want to attend. First, you need to make it interesting and different. It should be enjoyable. There should also be a structured format. You need to deliver some valuable information or content that they don't normally get that's going to make their lives better, their jobs easier, or their paychecks larger. There should be some benefit of the networking event other than just meeting a whole bunch of people. Don't make your group just like every other group—generic vanilla. If your group has a personality behind it, you have a real opportunity to grow the group of people who are truly going to be loyal to you, want to do business with you, and continue attending your networking events.

Technique 3: Bandit Signs

Bandit signs can be a very quick and affordable way to generate leads in a small, geographically targeted area. Bandit signs are the signs that you see on the side of the road with the little metal stands. They're typically 18 × 24 inches and are frequently brightly colored and have a message printed on them. For example, think of "For Sale By Owner" signs, "We Buy Ugly Houses" signs, or political campaign signs.

Because they're cheap, you can put many of them around your local area to create a stir and buzz for a particular offer for not much money. This is a great supplemental lead generation strategy if you're running other types of media in your market. If you're sending direct mail, if you're running ads on the radio, or if you're placing ads in a local publication, you can add bandit signs to the mix and intensify the frequency that people are exposed your message. Signs like these can also be very effective for promoting local special events like festivals, fairs, grand openings, or sale promotions.

Depending on the quantity you order, you can get them for as little as 73¢ apiece. The important thing to keep in mind about bandit signs is that they're not to be used the way that politicians use them—as an image builder, or a get-your-name-out-there tool. It's just another lead generation tool that should be used to make an offer for your free information, along with a web site preferably, or an automated phone number. Then you can take those leads and you can put them into your marketing funnel.

You don't want to make the information on the sign too wordy. You want to boil it down to the least common denominator so the words will be large on the sign. For example, "Free Report Reveals ———" or "Free 10 Minute Massage."

Businesses bandit signs are perfect for a business that is marketing to consumers inside a specific neighborhood or area within a five-by-five-mile radius.

You could place these all over the city, but you want to make sure to localize your signs so that people see them frequently as they drive around. One lone sign in an area isn't going to do any good. You want people to see it at every corner they come to, at every stop sign, at every turn.

Let's say you are a birthday party entertainer. You would put something like "Best Kid's Birthday Ever—Guaranteed. Free report at www.xyz.com." This is the formula.

In fact, if what you are offering has enough demand like lawn service, pool service, roof repair, drywall repair, or maid service, then there's already built-in needs and wants for those services. For example, if your roof has a leak, you want your roof fixed now. If the guy who cuts your lawn stops working in your area, you need someone else to cut your lawn. You want a new lawn service. If your maid leaves, you need a new maid.

It can be difficult to find small local businesses because they don't have the budget to market properly. You never even see them. If you need a lawn service, and you're driving around and see a sign that reads, "Cheap lawn service" with a phone number, you're likely to call it. If you saw "Don't get ripped off by your lawn guy" or "Best lawn service or it's free" or "Best looking lawn guaranteed!" you'd be even more likely to take action.

A little offer, maybe a guarantee, an offer for something for free, is the idea. You wouldn't want to try to target business owners with a bandit sign. You also wouldn't want to put your logo and your company name on the bandit sign.

Here's a perfect example of bandit signs being used properly. If your business has a physical location, such as a day spa that offers massages or a dance school for children, most likely people drive by all the time. These businesses should put bandit signs along the front of their location. But often they make a mistake because the sign they put out will be their company name and "Now Open." "Weight Loss for Women! Now Open" or "Absolute Perfection Day Spa, Now Open."

Instead you should put "Free massage—turn here!" or "Lose weight for free—turn here [web site, or phone number]." Everyone wants something free. People will turn in for something free.

If you use a web site, they don't even need to turn or stop. "Free massage—full details at www.xyz.com." People go to the web site, which reads, "We're a new day spa, we've just opened, and we're doing free 10 minute massages. We'd like to welcome you. We'd like to get to know our new neighbors. Come on in for a complimentary 10 minute chair massage."

You could also try, "Free massage coupon—www.xyz.com." When you do this, then the web page that they land on when they go to your web site can read, "You probably saw one of our signs. Here we are and here's what we do. Enter your contact information for your printable coupon for a free massage."

Another thing you have to realize about bandit signs is that they're going to be removed. The county and city will come and take your signs away. Competitors and kids will remove your signs. They will disappear. So they're very temporary. You have to be prepared to replace those signs, if in fact they're generating leads for you, which they should be. If they're not, you want to move those signs to locations that do generate leads for you. You don't want to just place signs and forget about them. You need to keep track of them so that you can find out if they're generating calls for you.

The big mistake you should avoid is relying on this small, cheap, disposable media to make the sale for you. Remember, all you want the bandit sign to do is to make the introduction for you. There has to be a hook and permit component to it.

$ Expert Resource

Doug Huggins is a nationally acclaimed mortgage and real estate marketing expert. His programs have been used across the country to help real estate professionals explode their businesses by attracting scores of eager home buyers and helping those buyers get the home of their dreams.

While running a near seven figure mortgage and real estate company, Doug used a wide array of lead attraction strategies all in a localized area. He is a master of using multiple lead attraction methods simultaneously, including bandit signs.

To learn about how Doug generated over 280 in-bound lead calls for 107 consecutive weeks, visit the Gravitational Marketing resource site at www.GravityBook.com/bandit.

Technique 4: Cold Calling

Cold calling is definitely our least favorite of all marketing options. We don't like cold calling because you get rejected, it takes a ton of time, everyone treats you like a jerk, you end up doubting yourself, questioning your own expertise, and it doesn't make you look like the expert that you want to be. But some people will insist on it anyway.

If you're trying to position yourself as an expert, being the guy on the phone making a cold call reduces your level of expert perception. In most cases, experts don't go hunting other people down. People come to them. So cold calling undermines this strategy, but in some cases cold calling can be effective. We have personally used it in some of our marketing efforts, but we weren't the people making the cold calls. We have other people make the cold calls and again, just like any other Gravitational Marketing approach, the cold call offers something for free.

The cold-call telemarketer makes an offer for a free widget. If the prospect accepts the offer, then that creates a relationship. The cold caller collects the prospect's contact information to mail them something free or invite them to an open house, a seminar, or a consultation. Whatever that free widget is that you're promoting to make that introduction, you can use cold calling to do it.

People like to believe that cold calling is free, but it is not. Even if you do it yourself you're giving up your time and that costs money. If you're not doing it yourself, which you shouldn't be, you're hiring someone else to do it. We've found that it can be a very effective tool, but it has a price tag, whether it's your time or the labor expense of having someone else do it.

Having said that, you want to be sure to develop and stick to a script. Without a script, the call is not going to work. There are plenty of cold-call experts out there who can tell you what that script should say. We've tried many different ones. They all work similarly. We have found typically that the less slimy the call's sales approach is and the more genuine the interest in giving away value is, the better the result.

Keep in mind that most cold-call scripts try to make a sale on the phone. Again, you want to be delivering value first with an offer for something free, a free next step.

A good example is what magazines do. They'll cold-call and say, "Mrs. Jones, I'd like to send you a complimentary food and wine tasting guide to help guide you through making food and wine purchase decisions and to tell you about the best of the best of all foods and wines. I'd like to send that to you absolutely free along with three free issues of *Food Delights* magazine. You'll pay nothing now, we'd just like to introduce you to this new magazine and give you this free gift. May we send it?" If the prospect agrees, they'll send the package and the free magazines, and then they'll continue sending the magazine along with the bill in the future.

Now, you're probably not in the magazine business, but you can learn from it. Typically, magazine companies give something away for free first. If it's a children's magazine, they'll give away children's books. Hunting magazines give away good luck coins, knives, hunting guides, and so forth. Food magazines give away food and wine reports. This is what we've been talking about—creating a free widget that can introduce your product or your service. You can offer that on the telephone. That's a much easier telemarketing call instead of calling to make the actual sale with an exchange of money.

The other thing you can do with cold calling is to try to generate leads on the phone, not by offering something for free, but by looking for interest. In this case, you try to set up a meeting. This is the favored, although hated, method of professional services companies.

They'll call around, business to business, and talk to other business owners trying to chat with them to find out if they can do a "needs assessment" to determine if that business owner needs what they are selling.

An excellent way to approach that without the normal, "Hey, can we get together for a needs assessment meeting?" is to conduct a small survey in your market about something your prospects might be interested in. You could offer to do some legwork for them in their particular business. This works especially well if you're trying to target multiple companies in the same niche or industry.

For example, maybe you sell to financial planners. You could perform research and do a survey about financial planning needs in the community. When you call your prospects, you could say, "Hey, my name is so-and-so, and I've done a survey on people's financial planning needs in our area. I would really love to share the data with you. Can we meet for lunch so that I can show you the data that I've collected?" This is going to be extremely interesting to prospects because you've done something that could help them in their business. You want to bring that to the table. You want to prethink the call before you pick up the phone and invite yourself to lunch with them for no reason. If there's no reason, it's obvious you're going to make a pitch. You always want to think about how you can deliver that value first.

Bonus Resource

Jim and Travis' Sample Cold Call Script
Cold calling is never fun but for it to be effective, you must use a script. Scripts are often overlooked and many business owners think they know their products well enough to wing it. That is a bad strategy, no matter how good you are. Our script can give you a head start on creating a cold call script with Gravitational Marketing elements built in.
Don't miss this little gift at www.GravityBook.com/bonus.

Technique 5: Sponsorships

Many people talk to us about sponsorships. They say, "Well, I've bought an ad in my church bulletin, or I have an ad in the program at my kid's high school musical, or I'm sponsoring a little league baseball team, or I'm paying for a table sponsorship at my chamber of commerce."

The first thing that we have to say about this is that we don't recommend planning for the sponsorship expense in your marketing budget. Instead, plan for it in your philanthropy budget. We recommend that you consider it as more of a donation than a marketing expense.

Typically, the results don't warrant the expense. But, if you have a kind heart and you would like to give back to the church, the school, the Little League, the chamber of commerce, or to whomever is asking you to sponsor their activity, then that is great.

If you decide that you want to do this, then you want to make sure the ad you place, or the sign you place, makes a hook and permit offer.

Let's say that you run a pool cleaning company, and you place a pool cleaning ad in a church bulletin that's the size of a business card. You don't want to place your business card in the ad. You also don't want to just put your company logo, name, or phone number. You need to say, "Have a crystal clear, sparkling blue pool 365 days a year. Learn how for free at www.SparklingPoolOrlando.com."

Technique 6: Trade Shows

Trade shows can be an excellent lead generation tool for the right kind of business. If you sell a product or service that is specifically geared toward an audience that gathers for meetings, conventions, or trade shows, you have an opportunity to show up, in person, and attract leads.

You can generate leads in mass quantities at trade shows and give a powerful boost to your marketing efforts.

Most exhibitors at trade shows completely squander the opportunity. They stand in their booth with their hands in their pockets and wait for people to come to them. People believe that just by appearing at a trade show they'll be solidifying their presence in the market ... getting their name out there. As with any other form of marketing, you must actively and aggressively cause prospects to come to you. No waiting around allowed.

Joel Bauer is one of the world's leading trade show attraction experts and has represented some of the largest companies on the planet. He offers the following four critical elements for trade show success.

He Who Is Loudest, Wins

If your message cannot be clearly heard on the trade show floor, you will lose the game of attendee attention and ultimately the dollars generated by that attention. It's in your best interest then to invest in a good 100-watt or more public address system with quality speakers and a headset microphone for your representative.

Eye Level Is *Buy* Level

If your products cannot be seen and dramatized, then you will fail. Raise all your products to counter levels of 55 to 75 inches so that the first person who stops to check out your offering isn't the only one who can see what it's all about. Don't underestimate this tip. It's mission critical to your sales success.

Place Your People on Pedestals

If your products must be seen, so too must the person demonstrating the key features and benefits of those products. Stand on a 2- to 20-inch riser and watch the effect this has on the attendees. An added psychological benefit to this boost in height is that as children we are used to looking up physically to people of wisdom. By standing on a riser, you put yourself in this position of sage authority.

Gifts and Prizes Secure Attention

Attendees are motivated to watch information-intensive demonstrations if they are assured that their attention will be rewarded. Stamp your company's logo on toys, T-shirts, wallets, pens, and sunglasses, and distribute these to attendees in exchange for their active attention to your pitch. Coupons for your services or product samples also make for top notch giveaways.

Attraction through Direct Mail

The post office provides the greatest marketing tool that has ever existed: direct mail. More money is spent every year on direct mail than on any other form of marketing. Direct mail is a marketing method that even the smallest company can use to obtain new customers and make extra money very quickly. You can begin using direct mail with very little money. And when it's done properly, achieving a return on your investment is simple.

How to Get Your Mail Opened

An important concept to understand before you begin to use direct mail is that people sort their mail over the garbage can. They quickly scan the pile of envelopes, magazines, postcards, and other printed matter and decide what they're going to give a second look and what they're going to put right in the can.

Drive into any apartment complex at the end of the day and watch the residents pick up their mail. You'll witness a mass dumping of junk mail. What does this mean for you? You can't afford to be caught in the junk mail pile. So how do you avoid it?

One very simple method is to make your mail look like something other than junk mail. Making your direct-mail piece look like a piece of personal mail is known as *sneak-up mail*.

Sneak-up mail involves:

- Using plain white No. 10 envelopes or colored invitation-size envelopes (see Figure 10.1).
- Affixing real first-class stamps (sometimes using something other than the standard, stamp, like a commemorative stamp).
- Addressing by hand or using realistic handwriting fonts.
- Avoiding the use of a business name in the return address.
- Making the letter resemble personal correspondence.

FIGURE 10.1 **Sneak-Up Envelope Example.** A sneak-up mail piece should look as much like personal mail as possible. Here is a good example of what a sneak-up style envelope should look like. Standard No. 10 envelopes that are hand addressed tend to be the most compelling to the recipient. A subtlety shown here is the use of a commemorative first-class postage stamp affixed slightly off kilter to give it a personal, done-by-hand look.

Another method is to make a powerful and bold offer on the outside of the envelope so that the recipient has a desire to open it even if they suspect it's a piece of solicitation. This method is known as *billboard mail*.

Billboard mail involves:

- Making big, bold promises on the outside of the envelope or on the front of the postcard.
- Encouraging the reader to open the envelope immediately.
- Conveying clear benefits.
- Relating the offer to a specific target.
- Using as much of the envelope or postcard space as possible.
- Offering something for free.

Both of these methods can be used with success. The method you should use largely depends on who your target is, what you're offering, and whether you have an existing relationship with the recipient. When in doubt, use the sneak-up approach because it's harder to screw up.

What Should Be inside the Envelope?

We're going to give you several techniques and tactics for using the mail effectively, but one standard premise exists in all applications: the more you tell, the more you sell. There is absolutely no reason to be brief.

Inside your envelope you want to be sure to include a powerful headline, a compelling story, a valuable offer, and a clear and easy way to respond. These elements should be present in every single direct-mail effort you make.

A typical direct-mail package contains a letter, a reply card, and a brochure for your product or service. But there are many variations on the same theme, some of which we'll discuss in this chapter.

What you should always keep in mind is this: Don't strive for perfection right out of the gate. If you wait around to perfect your mail piece before you send it, you will never send it. An *average* direct-mail piece that gets sent will always perform better than a *perfect* direct-mail piece that sits on your desk.

$ | **Expert Resource**

The goal at Specialized Mailing Services (SMS) is simple: get your message into the hands of your targeted audience and read, read immediately, a primary key to direct-mail success. SMS thrives under the leadership of Alice Mishica, a veteran of over 400 million specialized pieces and one of the country's leading experts in managing and getting creative direct mail opened and read.

We contract SMS exclusively when we need our mail piece to make a special impact, and we make extensive use of their services alongside an impressive list of other top marketers including Gary Halbert, Dan Kennedy, Jay Abraham, and Ted Nicholas.

(continued)

Whether it's tear sheets, hand addressing, odd shapes, or unique inserts, Alice and her SMS team are where the specialists turn for insight and direction. Considering a direct-mail concept? Make it a reality with Specialized Mailing Services! To learn more about the SMS team or Alice, visit www.GravityBook.com/sms.

What Kind of Results Should You Expect from Direct Mail?

Many people believe that direct mail does not work. Recently, one of our friends who is a marketing manager for a very respected company told us that he didn't want to use direct mail in his upcoming campaign because of the low response rates.

In truth, direct mail doesn't really perform any better or any worse than any other marketing media. But direct mail is criticized for its low response rates because the sender of a direct-mail campaign knows exactly how many people the letter was sent to—which means the sender can actually measure the response rate, unlike broadcast or print advertising when you never really know exactly how many people saw or read your ad.

Direct mail is a numbers game. Direct mail usually delivers a response in the neighborhood of 0.5 percent to 1 percent. That means for every one hundred letters that you send out, you will get one-half to one response. In some cases it is lower, and in other cases it is higher. Highly targeted campaigns yield a greater result. Campaigns sent to existing customers yield a higher result. But when mailing to a cold list of people you have never talked to before, a 0.5 percent to 1 percent response is what you can count on.

But that's not what really matters. Instead of measuring response rate, you need to concern yourself with ROI.

You may be wondering how you can possibly make money with a 1 percent response? This goes back to determining and understanding the value of a lead. If you recall the marketing funnel that we talked about earlier, you understand that every lead adds up. They go through your funnel, and some come out the other side as a sale. If you take your total sales volume and divide it by the total number of leads, you'll find out your value per lead. In many cases, we've found a single lead to be worth hundreds of dollars. If you send 1,000 letters at a cost of 85¢ each, you spend $850. If you get a 1 percent response, that is 10 leads. If they're each worth $500 to you, then the value of that mailing is $5,000. You only spent $850 to receive that value. So your return is about six times the amount of your investment, which makes it worthwhile.

It's not important how many people responded to your mail. What's important is how much money you made for every dollar you spent. If you send a direct-mail letter out to 5,000 people at a cost of $4,000, and you get a .5 percent response, you are only hearing back from 25 people. But what do those 25 people turn into for you? Do you end up doing business with five of them? And if so, how much money does that make for you? If you're in the mortgage business, and you make an average commission of $2,500 per closed loan, and you close five loans, your $4,000 investment will have blossomed into a $12,500 payday. That's a pretty good thing.

The Biggest Direct-Mail Mistake You Can Make

Here's how most people use direct mail: They send one letter. That's it. But one attempt does not make a direct-mail campaign. No mail campaign should be less than three steps in a sequence, and it could be as many as 12, 15 or 25 steps.

The standard rule for determining whether to send another piece to the same list of people is based on whether your last attempt made a profit. If you sent out 1,000 pieces and got enough response to cover your cost and make some money, mail again! Continue mailing until one of your mailings produces no ROI. But here's the caution: You need to be sure the poor response is not due to a list or copy problem. You also want to be sure there isn't an offer problem, meaning the message and the market don't match. These are reasons people might not be responding. If you determine that one of these things is the problem, you wouldn't want to send a second and third piece to that group. You want to make sure that you only send second, third, fourth, and fifth sequential pieces once you know that the list is good and your offer and piece are good. This way you can know you're getting a profitable response on each mailing.

Frequency in marketing causes a greater response up to a certain point of diminishing marginal return. So sending multiple direct-mail pieces causes recipients to see the same message more than once, thereby increasing the odds that they will respond. Plus, the first piece may never reach the person or may never be opened, where the second piece may. And if not the second, then the third.

How Many Pieces Should You Send?

What is the ideal size of a direct-mail list? On a test mailing, we wouldn't test with any more than 2,500 names. At the minimum, we would mail to a list of 500 because with 500 pieces sent, if you get a 0.5 percent response, that's only two or three people. If you send any less than 500, and you get a 0.5 percent response, that may result in zero leads and you may think that your mailing didn't work. But at 500, if the result is zero leads, you can be pretty sure that your mailing didn't work. You want to be sure the size of the mailing is large enough to be statistically valid.

From the Trenches

Here's an example of good marketing and a company that's not confused about getting its name out there.

My wife received an invitation to visit a retailer and choose five hand soaps for $10. This retailer has the exclusive on soap in my house, so my wife excitedly hurried down to their store the next time she was out.

When she arrived, they showed her some new scents of soaps and she really liked one of them. Of course, that new scent didn't fall into the five-for-$10 category, but this was not a problem.

The salesperson said, "Even though this soap is marked $9, you can package it with the others you've chosen for only $15." My wife comes home feeling like a champ, proudly displaying her new scented soaps and announcing that she was able to wrap a $9 bottle of soap in with these others and get five for just $15. Wow!

I thought to myself, "Who would ever believe we would buy $15 worth of soap at one time and come home feeling like we got a great deal?"

It's amazing, isn't it? You can buy a brick of 12 bars of generic soap for less than $2 at the discount store. You can buy a 64-ounce refill bottle of generic hand soap for a little more. That would last a year or two at my house. In fact, many people might price shop that brick of soap.

But this retailer has removed itself from the soap business. They don't sell soap. They sell an experience. They sell a show. They sell you the ability to wash your hands and feel like a big shot or a princess. They sell you the excitement of smelling new and exotic scents in your own bathroom. In that context, five for $15 is a bargain!

Is this soap any better than the generic soap? I don't know. I can't say. Is it seven times as good? Probably not. But they have shown that it doesn't matter.

The other thing at work here is the offer itself. This mailer didn't just show the product and display the name of the company alongside, "Buy me!" "Come in!" "We're the best!" or "Great customer service!" This mailer didn't even discuss the "experience" I mentioned earlier. This was a mailer to existing customers. It didn't need to. This mailer focused on one thing: the offer of five for $10.

(continued)

Many companies would be scared to make an offer like that. Many companies would prefer to get their name out there. If this mail piece wasted time getting their name out there, it would have been speaking only to the trash can, but an offer as strong as this one stopped my wife in her tracks.

Here we are back to the fact that $10 for a soap experience is a great offer. See how cyclical it is? See how one depends on the other? The experience speaks for itself. There's little need to say it out loud or on paper. People probably wouldn't believe it anyway. But the offer is real, believable, and specific. It speaks for the sale. The offer is what makes the ad work and the experience is what makes the offer work.

Here's the million dollar question: What should the mailer say if it was being sent to people who are not already customers? Here are a couple ideas and thoughts:

- "Free Soap Sampler Pack Just for Visiting."
- Don't send mail to noncustomers for an item this cheap unless you're certain you can get that customer back again and again.

Technique 7: Direct-Mail Letter

There are many myths about sending a direct-mail letter. One big myth is that the letter should be short. That isn't necessarily the case. In fact, we usually find that the opposite is true. The longer letters tend to sell better because they give the recipient a better understanding of your product or service.

A letter should be no different than what you would say to a person who was sitting in front of you about the reason why they should do business with you. The letter should sound like personal communication—a personal conversation back and forth between you and the reader of that letter.

Imagine writing a letter to your grandmother about a wonderful product or service you've experienced. This should be what a letter is like when you send it to someone to generate business for yourself.

It's not a standard business form letter or some flyer that you just put in the mail. It's not on your company letterhead. Most people think direct mail doesn't work because they've sent these ineffective types of letters before and have had very little response. A good direct-mail letter is like a salesman pitching to the reader on paper.

From the Trenches

Here's a recent real-life example of a small business, a car dealership in North Carolina, using letters to generate a tremendous ROI. When they recently opened a small satellite dealership, they expected to have many customers. Instead, they had an empty showroom. Nobody was coming. They waited, and they waited. The dealer, who had learned from us about the power of sending direct-mail letters, decided to write a letter introducing himself and his dealership in a very casual, noncorporate manner, which was to be sent to new people who had moved into the area. He also offered a free gift—a set of knives.

He mailed his two-page letter that was very simply written to 2,500 people. As he had learned from us, he expected that he might get about 1 percent of the people to show up, maybe 25 people in all. He actually had over 100 people come in for those knives. Many of those people ended up test driving a vehicle and he sold enough vehicles to make more than $50,000 in profit. His entire investment for marketing was about $2,500 and he multiplied that into a return of 20 times that. That's a tremendous ROI, using a low-tech, low-cost method that was simple, quick, and easy. The beautiful thing is that he now has a scheduled monthly mailout to the new people who move into the area.

Technique 8: Endorsed Mailing

An *endorsed mailing* is when a company or individual sends a letter to their clients, friends, or family on your behalf, recommending or endorsing you. Typically, you pay for the endorsed mailing, but it appears on their stationery or letterhead and is written in their voice as if it's coming from them. This is extremely powerful because it essentially acts as a testimonial, with them saying that they have used your product or service and that they want to recommend it to the recipients. There is virtually no higher or better form of marketing than this, and for the new business owner who is just getting started or the existing business owner who needs a boost, this can be one of the most pure, powerful, and effective methods you can employ.

> An endorsed mailing allows you to capitalize on existing relationships generated by someone else.

This game is all about goodwill and trust. This person has a group of clients, customers, friends, and family members who know, like, and trust him. Now that you've made a relationship with him, his group feels that you and your service or product is credible. So they're going to tell their friends, customers, and family members about you and what you can do for them. This is really significant in terms of marketing because the people you're going to be reaching will be far more receptive to the message when it comes from someone they trust and hear from regularly. This is key.

The person you do the endorsed mailing with, who has the client base, needs to be someone who has a strong relationship with those clients, not someone who doesn't speak to them on a regular basis. If not, you might as well be sending the mailing to a cold list of people who neither of you have ever talked to before. You need to find someone who has a good relationship with their prospects and their customer list, and then piggyback on their respect, trust, and reputation.

Let's say you're a web site designer, and you'd like to get new clients. After you've done a good job for a client and developed a new web site that she's particularly pleased with, you would ask your client, "How would you like to present your customers with a very valuable opportunity as a gift from you?" She would say, "Yes, that sounds quite nice."

Let's pretend that you are speaking with a business consultant. You'd propose, "I'd like to offer every single one of your clients a free web site for 30 days as a gift from you. I'd like you to write a letter, or I'll write it for you, that expresses how pleased you were with the new web site that I designed for you and the dramatic benefits that your company has seen as a result of this new web site. Then tell the story about how you've arranged for each of them to have a web site for free for 30 days. It will make you look like the hero. They'll love you for it. How would you like to do that? I'll pay for the entire mailing. We'll just use your stationery and it will be written as if it's coming from you. I'll take it to the post office and I'll do all the work."

It's a win-win situation for both parties because you as the web site designer are getting a chance to promote yourself. The business consultant is getting an opportunity to provide something of value to her client base, which makes her look good, but she doesn't have to do any work or spend any money. It's a symbiotic relationship that works out well for both people.

In most cases, we recommend to our clients that they write the letters for the partner. Otherwise, the partner may never get around to writing the letter and it's very important for you to get this endorsed mailing off the ground. That is why you should do all the legwork. The only thing they need to do is give you the mailing list, provide the stationery for you to print the letters on, and okay the letter once it's written. That is how you would perform an endorsed mailing and it works very well.

The offer could be anything of value. It could be a report. It could be a phone consultation about the Internet, web sites, marketing, and how to increase your monthly income using those tools. All kinds of things can be done with an endorsed mailing, but the key is to find someone who has a list of clients and a relationship with those clients that can benefit you.

Technique 9: Cannonball Mailing

If the value of a customer for you is high enough and the market is small enough, then a strategy that we call *cannonball mailing* can be used. Here is a perfect example. Let's say you're a speaker and want to target the CEOs of companies that do between $10 million and $50 million per year and have more than 50 employees. You know that you're never going get a direct-mail letter through to that CEO. You know that there are so few CEOs like that in the world that you couldn't possibly reach them on the radio, television, or in the newspaper. Regardless, you need the CEO to contact you because you want to get hired as a speaker, consultant, or whatever it is that you do.

To employ this cannonball mailing strategy, you buy the mailing list of these CEOs and send them a package that could never be missed. This is perfect if you need to reach people whose mail is screened and opened for them because you know that a junk mail letter would never make it to them. You might send a box, a package, or a huge, amazing item.

Let's say you're a dentist who wants to target the above mentioned CEOs. You might send a huge, oversize toothbrush to the CEO along with a little note that explains why you're the dentist that CEO should see.

Let's say you do cosmetic dental work. In this case, you could send a very large set of perfect teeth. Imagine them being several feet wide. If you mail somebody a huge set of dentures like this, which by the way you can find at novelty web sites online, when they arrive from an overnight delivery service, chances are pretty great that they will reach the CEO. A huge toothbrush or a huge set of teeth will almost certainly reach its destination because it's not another piece of junk mail. The cost to send these items can be high per piece, but if the transaction value is high enough and the importance of reaching this person is high enough, then this may make sense.

It is also very important to note, we always recommend sending these packages through an overnight delivery service. It helps separate your package further from the junk mail.

You may have heard of the concept of lumpy mail. This is what would be considered really lumpy mail, but you can send smaller items as well in different types of packaging to get similar results. There are even companies out there that will print your custom message on a ball that can be mailed just as the ball, not in any envelope or packaging. That is sure to get attention.

We also have clients who have sent DVD players in an overnight box with the sales message on a DVD inside the player. When this package arrives, all the prospect has to do is take the DVD player out and there's a sticker that reads, "press this button." The batteries are in the DVD player already. They press the button and the sales message comes on. That's a more costly mailing, so of course you want to make sure that your transaction value is going to be high and the recipient is going to be qualified when you send a piece like that.

We did another campaign for a professional speaker who wanted to target high-level companies. For him, we wrote a letter offering a one-on-one private executive training session. We sent this letter along with a large admission ticket, like one you would see for a high school sports event. You may be imagining those small red tickets. The tickets we sent were more like two feet by three feet.

When something like that comes into the office, you cannot miss it. It stands out and gets people's attention. This is a very powerful strategy to use when you're trying to target a small group of people with a high transaction value.

Let's say because you're using such an amazing piece and such a targeted list you can get a 10 percent response. This is reasonable. Imagine that it cost you $50 to send this particular package. You sent one hundred of these packages, so the mailing cost you a total of $5,000. At a 10 percent response, you got 10 replies. You're a professional speaker and you know that for every 10 companies you speak with you'll book two events. If your average event pays you $10,000, then this single $5,000 mailing with 10 replies would result in booking two events making you $20,000. This was a good ROI.

This strategy is also very effective for business-to-business companies that sell high-tech items. The companies make many thousands of dollars for each sale, but it can be very hard to reach the target. This strategy helps you get through to the decision maker and puts something very visible on his or her desk.

We've even seen people send $100 bills attached to their sales message through an overnight delivery service to get their prospect's attention. This stuff works very well. It takes a little bit of chutzpah to run a program like this but from an effectiveness point of view it stands out and gets results.

$	**Expert Resource**

Mitch Carson is a man you want to have in your rolodex. He can help you get your mail opened and acted on. A 20 minute conversation we had with Mitch saved us from making a $10,000 mistake. His systems for using object mail will skyrocket your direct-mail response rates and have your prospects buzzing about you.

Direct mail can be tricky, and Mitch can guide you through the process and show you the campaigns that have been home runs for the countless businesses he has consulted with.

To learn more about how to maximize your mail efforts, raise your ROI, and make an impact with your next direct-mail campaign, hightail it over to the Gravitational Marketing resource site at www.GravityBook.com/Mitch.

Technique 10: Postcards

Postcards are very popular these days, and they are elected many times by smaller businesses as the preferred direct-mail method because they're cheap to print and mail. Many people choose them because there's not a lot of space on them in their traditional form, so they don't have to write much. In addition, there are companies that have preprinted postcards. All you have to do is choose one and mail it.

Postcards can be effective. They typically have a lower response rate than a direct-mail letter, but they also cost less, so the ROI could be positive. Postcards generally work better for business-to-consumer applications than for business-to-business applications.

Many people are locked into traditional postcards. They think a postcard mailing has to be the size of the postcard that you get off the rack, which is typically a quarter of a page. They think it should have a glossy photograph on it and feature a cute saying.

That isn't necessarily the case. In our experience, we've found that going against the traditional postcard approach tends to work better. When we say *against* we mean no full-color glossy photo on one side, instead a lot of sales-based copywriting all over the postcard and sizes that are not standard so they seem different and look different in the pile of mail. Typically, small postcards get lumped in with all the junk mail and end up going right into the trash.

One of the benefits of a postcard is that it's not inside an envelope, so regardless of whether it's on its way to the trash can or sitting in a pile; the person has a chance to get the message without having to examine it in depth or open an envelope. The key to a postcard, just like the key to any advertisement, is to get the person's attention with a large headline that will cause them to pick up the postcard and examine it further before it heads to the trash can.

The headline should not be a cute, creative little saying based on the photo that's on the card. It should communicate a huge benefit or a free offer that the person receiving that postcard would want. It should give them something to enhance their lives, their position in life, and their position in their profession or make them more money. It should convey some huge benefit.

We've done postcards in every size imaginable. We like odd sizes like long rectangles and full-size $8\frac{1}{2} \times 11$ inch postcards. We've even done postcards that are 11×17 inches folded in half with four panels of full copy, which have been highly effective (see Figure 10.2).

From the Trenches

Here are two stories of our experiences sending postcards at two different times and the very different reactions we got to them. One time we chose to send a quarter-page postcard that was

(continued)

glossy. It had a photograph on the front that had a cute and clever theme, and it offered a free widget, which happened to be a free teleseminar. We sent it to 10,000 people in a particular business category, and only had two of them respond and register for the teleseminar. That is what we call failure. That was a miserable disaster and waste of money. It didn't work, and we did not have the teleseminar.

In another instance, we sent another postcard that offered a teleseminar. This time, it was not glossy. It was on brightly colored yellow paper. It didn't have pictures. It had a big bold headline. We filled every inch of that yellow postcard with black text on both sides. We sent it to a group of people in another business industry. This time we sent it to about 7,000 people. This postcard was a long rectangle, about 5 inches tall by about 11 inches long and because of its odd shape it stood out in the mailbox. It couldn't get shuffled away with all of the other mail. No matter which way you turned it, it would stick out. We had 250 people register for that teleseminar.

Look at the massive difference in response that can happen. Two different postcards offering the same basic thing can have a difference in response of over one hundred times.

On another occasion, a client we worked with sent one of the small, glossy type postcards. He was trying to generate leads for a live seminar. The results were far and few between. The results were dismal compared to the same exact offer sent in a letter.

When Should You Send a Postcard

Some marketing gurus recommend sending postcards to do what's called *cleaning your list.* They say you should use a postcard to do this because they're cheap. These days you can send a postcard first class for about 26¢, and they're relatively cheap to print. When you mail your postcards, any with bad addresses will be returned to you, which allows you to remove those names and addresses from your mailing list before you mail a more expensive piece like a letter or package.

FREE ACCESS to Doug Huggins - **Tuesday, May 22nd, at 12:00 PM EASTERN** - The Nation's TOP Marketing Consultant Specializing In Purchase Money Mortgage Business ... And The Guy Who Generated Over 260 INBOUND Purchase Money Lead Calls For Over 107 Consecutive Weeks.

"What's Working NOW: How To Skyrocket Your Mortgage Business And Make An Additional $100,000.00 While Making Your Competition Look Minor League...GUARANTEED"

"Industry Insiders and LOs Across The Globe Are Crying Like Babies ... (That's OK) ... The first 101 LOs and Brokers Pre-Registered For My FREE Teleconference Will Be Exposed To The Real Truth About Making An Extra 100k .... (Even In Today's Troubled Climate) And Will Be Laughing All The Way To The Bank!"

FREE TELECONFERENCE REVEALS: How To Make An Additional 100K In Your Mortgage Business In The Next 12 Months The Embarrassingly Simple And Easy Way.

Here's what you'll discover during this revealing 45 minutes:

· How to position yourself as "THE" expert in your area and the only logical choice to do business with (this system makes your competition look minor league)

· How to "target" certain types of desirable buyers and get them to call you

· How to build a business that is enjoyable, simple and prosperous

· How to create more leisure time so you can play

more golf or do the things you love more often

· How to produce an ever-green stream of highly qualified leads

· The 4 questions you MUST ask every prospect before you even get their name (or quote rates or fees)

· How a desperate, dead-broke, 39 year-old single mother of 3 in New Jersey went from starving on food stamps to being a top loan producer—closing over $5 million in loans per month in just 57 days

· How to remove yourself from the "lowest rate" game, escape price competition and avoid cutting your fees just to keep a deal

· How to immobilize rate shoppers and spin them into raving fans after they've paid more in fees than they could have paid somewhere else

(please turn over)

100k Extreme Makeover

PRESORTED
FIRST CLASS
U.S. POSTAGE
PAID
PERMIT NO.

FREE TeleConference — Tuesday, May 22nd
12:00 pm Eastern / 11:00 am Central / 10:00 am Mountain / 9:00 am Pacific

---

So Why Am I Doing This Teleconference For NADA, ZERO, FREE?

I'm sure you're asking yourself...why is a guy like me who has basically retired from this business, travels the country teaching mortgage and real estate professionals how to grow their business and gets paid HUGE sums of money to consult, giving away his time for a free seminar?

Let me be blunt about my answer! I am doing this to spite the "Sub-Prime Debacle" and to show our industry critics that loan officers and mortgage brokers are fighters and won't go silently into the night.

Wanna know how I really feel about this Sub-Prime Mess? You'll laugh when I tell you how you can actually profit from it.

You see, I've been in this business a long time. I'm 55 years old. I've been a licensed real estate agent since 1972 and have run a highly successful, multi-million dollar mortgage and real estate company with 9 agents and 25 loan officers on staff.

What's funny is...those of you who get on this call will be the ones who will discover what you can do to whip your competitors who are complaining by the water cooler, looking for another career and asleep at the switch. A lot of guys in our business right now are taking an @#$* whoppin' and crying home to mama!

YOU DON'T HAVE TO DO THAT. It doesn't have to be your fate. I can show you how to turn it around. I've been around the block a few times. I've seen all the dips and dives the market has to offer over the years. And you know what? I've always found a way to not only survive but THRIVE.

Here's the thing. The market can throw whatever at me and I don't care. Been there, done that and got the T-shirt to prove it. My wife tells me it's not the age, it's the

mileage. And I've done Hard Time in this business and if my expertise can help just one of you hang in there it's worth my time to do this call.

So here's what I'm gonna do. In the final 10 minutes of the call I will reveal the #1 killer secret that will allow you to keep your head above water and at the same time allow you to make an additional 100k in the next 12 months. And you won't spend a dime!

Sound fair? Good.

Warning: Pass Up This Free Teleconference Only If You Want To Go Out Of Business

Are you doing what you've always done and getting the same or worse results? If you think something different is going to happen then you're insane. In fact, that's the definition of insanity (look it up). If you don't want to do something different then don't pre-register for this call. If you want to make more money in the next 12 months and give this industry and all its pundits a big fat smack in the face then be one of the 101 people to resister for this FREE TELECONFERNCE.

Only if you are serious about growing your business even though times are tough and are ready to try a different approach, visit:

www.100kExtremeMakeover.com/telecon

You will get all the call details via email.

FREE TeleConference
Tuesday, May 22nd

12:00 pm Eastern   10:00 am Mountain
11:00 am Central   9:00 am Pacific

What Other Mortgage Professionals Are Saying About Doug's Secrets Revealed On This Call...

"I wanted to tell you I hit pay dirt with just 1 idea from you. I got a $685,000 purchase ... $17,000 front end and back end points." —**Edward Russo, FL**

"The marketing techniques that you teach helped skyrocket my production from 4 closings per month to 8-10 closings per month in less than 60 days." —**Stanley Marshall, GA**

"If someone CAN'T make money with this information they are either asleep and doing nothing or are completely incompetent." —**Kris Wales, WA**

SPECIAL FREE BONUS GIFT

As my way of rewarding the 101 who are fast action takers and the upper echelon of this industry you'll also receive a very valuable and "RARE" SURPISE that is guaranteed to make you more money this year. This FREE Surprise will be sent to all 101 Teleconference attendees who join me on the call. I'll reveal what that Surprise is at the end of the call.

A "DON'T DELAY" REMINDER: I've sent this invitation to thousands of other LOs and brokers, but only 101 will be allowed to join the call for FREE.

Go online to: 100kExtremeMakeover.com/telecon to get the special Teleconference Hotline Phone Number and Access Code so you don't miss out.

Anyone who wants to be on the call after the first 101 will have to pay $99 to attend the call. Don't miss out on your FREE opportunity to hear this life changing information.

FIGURE 10.2   Effective Postcard. The front (top) of an inexpensive lead attraction postcard. Notice every inch of usable space is filled with selling copy. We should also point out the use of powerful headlines, bold offers, and the fun-natured picture to make it personal. This postcard measures 5 × 11 inches. The back (bottom) of the same lead attraction postcard. Again filled with selling copy and even a bonus offer for taking our predefined action.

Now, we don't always agree with that concept. Yes, postcards are the cheapest way to clean your list. However, sometimes postcards can have such a low response rate compared to a letter that even if you sent the letters, which cost more, you would still have netted more money by sending that letter than you would have by sending the postcard. And you would have cleaned your list at the same time.

What's important is to test the same offer in a letter and in a postcard side-by-side to find out which one works better for your audience or target. Having said that, all direct mail should be sent as a sequence, never as a singular piece. One letter is not a good idea. One postcard is an even worse idea. In the sequence of mailing to people, you may mail a letter, a postcard, then another letter, then a bigger postcard, then another letter, and then an even bigger postcard. You send different types, shapes, sizes, and colors so that people who respond differently all get an opportunity to react to different types of communication from you.

Postcards can be an important, valuable, and powerful tool. The best way to use a postcard is to offer something for free. A postcard will almost never be able to actually conjure a sale because there's not enough space to actually make the case unless you're using one of those 11 × 7 inch, folded in half, two-page, four-panel postcards we talked about. But they can be used to generate leads.

Another way to use a postcard is to reiterate and support a campaign that's already in place. This would be in a case where you've already sent a letter, and now you're going to send a postcard to reiterate what you said in the letter. Perhaps you want to remind them of a deadline or an opportunity that you've already made to them in the letter where you had more space to make your case.

Technique 11: Tear Sheet

A *tear sheet* is an article or advertisement disguised to look like a magazine or newspaper article that has been torn out, folded up with a sticky note placed on it by the sender.

All of the traditional rules of direct mail we've discussed so far apply here. The big difference between a tear sheet and other types of mail is that a tear-sheet mailing is even more covert. It tries to disguise itself as something sent by a friend who thinks you may be interested in it.

Generally, the sticky note, which is on the newspaper or magazine article, has a short message and an initial on it. The whole thing is folded and stuck into an envelope. Most often, the envelopes are standard No. 10, hand addressed, and mailed with a real stamp. Sometimes they are invitation-size envelopes made to look like a wedding invitation or a birthday card.

In other words, a tear sheet appears to be a newspaper article that's been written about you or your company, torn out by a friend or family member, and sent to you as a recommendation. But this is something that you create yourself by having a designer lay out a newspaper or editorial style advertisement for you. It has a headline on top; it has copy. It's about the benefits that come from your product or service, and it makes your offer for free information. It doesn't attempt to make the sale.

There are many companies that can print on newsprint to produce your tear sheets. Your tear sheets can then be sent to a mail house, which will fold them and add the sticky note. They handle it all.

The sticky note might say something like, "Jim, thought you'd be interested. This really works. J." J happens to be the most popular letter when it comes to first initials, so we always sign off with J. That makes it seem like someone they knew with the first initial J folded the sheet up and put it in an envelope and sent it to tell them about your wonderful offer.

The reason tear sheets work is because they're unique. People rarely receive them. They are perceived to be news instead of advertising or marketing. Also, they almost work as a third-party endorsement. You get some of the benefits of endorsed mailing that we talked about earlier. Another benefit is that you can use more copy because you're filling a page, an entire newspaper article, with information about your free offer.

One thing you need to know about tear-sheet mailings is that you must put an advertisement slug at the top of the tear sheet. This is a little caption that says, "advertisement." It does seem counterintuitive to the concept of being covert, but in order to comply with Federal Trade Commission regulations, you must include it. The good news is we've found that it does not diminish the response. It seems to have no negative effect.

Tear sheets can be used for business-to-business and business-to-consumer marketing. They work across the board in all business types (see Figure 10.3).

$ **Expert Resource**

Scott Tucker is a leading expert when it comes to profitable marketing for mortgage brokers. The campaigns he created for his personal mortgage brokerage made him a top producer, and now he licenses those exact same systems to mortgage professionals across the country.

His campaigns have been featured in countless magazines including *Consumer Reports* and he has been sought out by top industry professionals to create similar campaigns in other industries.

His stuff is devastatingly effective, and one of his most powerful tactics is the use of the tear-sheet mailing concept. Scott has put everything he knows about tear sheets for the mortgage business into his proven marketing system for loan officers and mortgage brokers.

To get more information on putting together highly profitable tear-sheet mailings, visit the Gravitational Marketing resource site at www.GravityBook.com/tearsheet.

Technique 12: Coupon Packs and Card Decks

Everyone's familiar with coupon packs in the mail. You have also probably received a thick, glossy, coated card deck in your home mailbox.

Local Harvard MD "rats out" billion-dollar financial firms

Central Florida doctor uncovers a conspiracy that robs other physicians of their wealth.

By JAMES VENEZIO
SYNDICATED COLUMNIST

ORLANDO - Thirteen years ago, local physician Josh Helman graduated from Harvard Medical School and discovered a problem. Due to the ballooning costs of malpractice insurance, sue-happy patients and terrible financial advice, practicing medicine is not the lucrative, fulfilling job he thought it would be.

This startling realization prompted Dr. Helman to seek the truth behind why so many doctors are being robbed of their wealth.

A bold move was necessary to unearth the answers. In his quest for the truth Dr. Helman decided to go incognito to find out first hand what was going on with the industry that supposedly helped physicians create and protect their wealth.

AN INDUSTRY EXPOSED

In January of 2003 Helman was hired and trained as a financial representative for one of the oldest and largest financial firms in the country, and what he learned was *shocking*.

"You see these big Wall Street firms and their army of product-peddling brokers have billion-dollar marketing budgets to train and brainwash people into believing that their off-the-

being withheld from the general public - or at least squelched by the huge marketing weight of Wall Street.

Their conspiracy theory led them to Mark Matson, CEO of Abundance Technologies, an

DR. JOSHUA HELMAN: Harvard MD dedicated to exposing truth kept from the medical community.

investment coaching company managing $1.5 billion (and growing by $1 million per day).

"We reveal 60 years of research - by professors of finance and

Based on these discoveries, Dr. Helman and Mr. Brooks started Xexis, Inc. (pronounced Ex Sis), a private wealth coaching company based in Heathrow, Florida.

To date Mr. Brooks and Dr. Helman, in cooperation with Mr. Matson, have authored two books, *Lies My Broker Told Me (and 101 Truths About Money and Investing)* and *The Investor Awareness Guide*. Their insights have graced the pages of *USA Today, Financial Services Advisor, Advisor Today* and others.

STILL PRACTICING MEDICINE

Dr. Helman hasn't given up his medical career totally, but he only practices a few days per month as an emergency room doctor for the University of Florida.

Outside of the ER, Dr. Helman and Mr. Brooks teach physicians all they have discovered and the little-known investment secrets the super-wealthy use to become and stay super-wealthy.

These secrets give their clients the edge they need to avoid the carefully-laid traps that can unexpectedly steal their wealth right out from under them.

OPPORTUNITY FOR OTHER PHYSICIANS

Dr. Helman and Mr. Brooks hold a "by reservation only" workshop entitled *Lies My Broker Told Me (and 101 Truths About Money and*

"You see these big Wall Street firms and their army of product-peddling brokers have billion-dollar marketing budgets to train and brainwash people into believing that their off-the-shelf, one-size-fits-all products are going to help you amass a king's ransom. But the truth is that much

FIGURE 10.3 **Example of a Tear Sheet.** A tear-sheet mailing looks like a newspaper article that has been torn out and mailed to a friend. Generally sent with a sticky note attached, it is meant to get past people's junk mail detector. This is an example of how a tear sheet should look.

Usually you see ads for stuff like garage floor refinishing, cabinet refinishing, or curb appeal stuff for your garden or home. These usually come wrapped in cellophane. For people selling consumer products, these can be valuable.

It's not great for business-to-business marketing. Although there are some business-to-business card decks out there, we haven't had a lot of success or experience with them, so we can't personally recommend them, but we do highly recommend the consumer card decks.

We recommend card decks because they are highly targetable by zip code or by neighborhood type. When writing your ad, keep in mind that people who are looking through the card decks are really treating them as coupons. They're looking for a discount, a special offer, or a sale.

We always tell marketers that it is better to bonus than to discount. What we mean by this is that you should give more value as a purchase incentive rather than cut your price. When it comes down to it, most people seem like they're price shopping, but they're only price shopping because there's no buying preference.

If you give them a buying preference and then a bonus on top of that, they're going to be more likely to choose you for the same amount or more money.

Always go with a bonus over a discount. But if you are going to discount, you better provide an extremely good reason for the discount that people can buy into. If you're just discounting for the sake of discounting, people may assume that you were overcharging or that the product isn't worth what you normally charge.

11

Attraction through Print

Print advertising can be an extremely effective tool for lead attraction. In fact, in many instances it's our preferred method for several reasons:

- Print advertising is easy to buy.
- It's plentiful.
- There are many different options.
- It is very scalable.
- It's easy to work print into just about any marketing budget because there are very affordable options as well as more expensive options.

In addition, print advertising is very targetable. There are many different varieties of audiences and niches that can be reached through print advertising. You can target people very narrowly, and the people who read the ads can be very receptive and responsive.

Through all of our advertising experience, we have found paid media placement in print publications to be the second least expensive form of lead generation in terms of cost per lead, falling just behind online methods (of course, this is barring any manual labor type of lead generation like networking or cold calling). But we typically find that leads generated from print advertising are a much higher quality than those generated online. For those reasons, print is often our first choice.

Another advantage we have found with print media is that the audience immediately gives you credibility just because your ad appears in the publication they are reading. Even though it's advertising, they still associate you with the publication they read and trust. The fact that you're in there immediately assigns that trust to your marketing. People very much believe what they read in print as compared to what they see on the television, hear on the radio, or even see on the Internet. Print media is a trusted source.

Another thing we really like about print media is that you have the ability to make your advertisements mimic the content of the media itself. People read newspapers and magazines for the articles. They watch television for the programming. They listen to the radio for the music. But only with print do you have the opportunity to make your advertisement look like the content of the media—in this case a magazine or a newspaper. In other words, you have the opportunity to make it look like an article. This gives your ad an automatic boost in credibility that you generally can't get with other media types.

When a commercial airs during a television program, everyone knows it's a commercial. When the music stops on the radio and a commercial begins, everyone knows it's a commercial. To get production values high enough for a radio spot to sound like music or for a television commercial to look like a show, you would have to spend an exorbitant amount of money. That can make the marketing uneconomical.

That leads us to one of our favorite attributes of print advertising, which is that it's pretty low cost to develop the ads, not including the copywriting. A low-cost graphic designer can do the actual production of the ads, or in many cases you can do them yourself on your computer. Another bonus is that the publication will often lay your ads out for you if you provide them with the copy and a sketch of what you are trying to make it look like.

What Should Your Print Ad Look Like?

When you begin thinking about what you want your print ad to look like, remember that you want your ad to look like an article. Don't make your ad look like an ad. If you use the same type style and mimic the look and feel of the rest of the magazine, in a lot of cases, people will read your ad thinking it's just another article. This gives your ad more credibility. We call these *advertorials*—an ad that looks like editorial content.

Open the newspaper or magazine in which you're thinking about placing an ad, and examine how the articles look. Each article probably features a headline, and it probably uses a certain font style, size, and column structure. It could be two, three, four, or maybe just one column. The columns may be justified. Typically, articles contain a photo and a caption. The paragraphs may be indented. You should try to mimic the look of the articles in the publication exactly.

There is one exception. In a world of color, black and white stands out. In a world of black and white, color stands out. If it's a color magazine, run a black-and-white ad. And if it's a black-and-white publication, use color so that your article stands out. You want to take every opportunity to stand out but at the same time look like content, not like advertising.

Another tip is to write your advertisement in an editorial style. This means it should read as if it were written by a third-party writer instead of by the advertiser. You don't want it to sound as if you're boasting about your own product or service.

Don't be fooled into thinking that you should not ask for the next action step in your advertorial. You must ask people to take the next step at the end of this editorial content. This is unlike a normal article that you would see in a newspaper or magazine. If you want to see what we're talking about, just pick up any *USA Today* and flip through it. There's always an advertorial-style ad somewhere in the paper. For example, take a look at Figure 11.1.

A common mistake with print advertising is that people try to make the entire sale in the advertisement. If the product or service you're selling costs more than about $30, then it's probably not a good idea to try to make that sale on paper. Instead, you should make your free offer. This way the people who read your ad, who are interested in the solution that you're talking about, will identify themselves to you by requesting your free widget.

Also, some people may mistakenly believe that print advertising should be used as a brand-building tool or as a tool to get their name out there. These people think putting their company logo or name in print will cause readers to remember them when they have a need for what they offer. Instead, you should make sure that you use print as a direct response media specifically asking people to take the next step. Do not leave it to chance. Do not make it a cute, frivolous ad or article about you. Instead, make your offer, and give them the reason to take the next step. You've got to have a call to action in the ad or it's worthless.

To Reps Who Want To Quit Work Someday...FREE Money Making Tool Kit Reveals...

How To Make An Extra $200,000 (or more) This Year With Your Existing Experience & Relationships...

...While Improving Your Credibility & Position In The Community, Helping Your Friends, With Absolutely No Investment, No Cold Calling, No MLM, No Hype & No BS

BY: JAMES VENEZIO

Benjamin Franklin, once said: "Wealth is not his that has it, but his that enjoys it." Oh, how true!

The accumulation and enjoyment of true wealth does more for a man's happiness and peace of mind than any other accomplishment in life.

And if you could use a biggie-size helping of happiness and peace of mind in your life right now, please read on for a few more moments.

In this article I'm going to whisk you on a millionaire's tour of a vast and wondrous universe of the lifestyle that could be yours!

I'm talking about **soaring across the country in a private jet**, stopping along the way to savor the local food and culture whenever you feel like it. Or living in an historic building downtown in the kind of apartment you only see in the movies. How about dining with aristocracy in the most exclusive private clubs and winding down the evening with the finest cigars and cognac? That's just a normal day in my life. Or maybe for you, enjoying wealth means sending your children to the finest private schools, providing security beyond your days, leaving a legacy while you live a legacy.

You see, as Franklin said, it's not only important to have wealth but to enjoy wealth. I'm prepared to teach you how to do both. Don't thank me...I have selfish reasons for it which I'll explain in a moment.

I assure you, *what I am about to tell you is going to change your outlook and enjoyment of life* more than anything you've ever experienced.

Let My Lifestyle Become Yours

My name is Kevin Schmidt and I used to be a dirt poor Louisiana boy struggling to make ends meet. I've hung drywall, dug ditches, fixed roofs, and worked in construction. I'll tell you upfront, I'm a first semester college drop out and I didn't grow up with a silver spoon in my mouth. More than likely, you're probably

smarter than I am. The problem is that I make a heck of a lot more money than you do...

You see, even though I didn't start with much, I figured out early in life that the guy who controls the purse strings is in control...the guy with the money is the most popular person in the room. Nowadays that person is me.

See, I got into the business of helping people get the money they needed or wanted. But it's not all about the money, it's what the money can do for people...grow their business...make their dreams come true.

Money Is Freedom

The world of venture capitalists, equity injectors, angels, investors and wealthy hotshots looking for deals to put their extra cash into is a secret, mysterious and private world that everyone wishes they could tap in to.

Imagine what having a personal relationship with someone like that could do for your life and the lives of the people around you.

I'll tell you...*people would gravitate to you*, they would want to be around you and do business with you, they would ask for your advice and respect what you had to say. You would be a beacon of hope and for growth and for prosperity.

That's exactly what life is like for me these days!

But Don't Envy Me...Join Me

Until now this unique and rare world of high-end lending and investing has been kept under a tight lid. That is until I decided to be *selfish and generous* at the same time.

The one thing I need now more than ever is new introductions to good people, smart business men and women, who need money to grow or expand, to build a new facility, or to invest in their dreams.

So I'm looking for a small group of reps to help me by making those introductions. And in the process, you can make a hearty portion of all the proceeds *(think of it as a finder's fee)* and be the
ADVERTISEMENT

go-to guy in your home town.

The best news is that it doesn't require any risk or manual labor or investment capital on your part. *I can set you up to make hundreds of thousands of extra dollars per year* by introducing your friends and business acquaintances to me...and my money.

Think about your position in the community and how much more influential and powerful you could be if you were the go-to guy for millions of dollars of dream fulfillment money.

And you make a huge additional income stream by helping others get what they want. As Zig Ziglar said, "You can get anything in the world you want if you help enough other people get what they want." I want to give you the resources you need to make that a reality.

This article is your invitation to join me on a journey of discovery of unsurpassed wealth building excitement and enjoyment that will be a true adventure of a lifetime.

I'd like to send you my money-making toolkit, at my expense, so that you can learn more about the opportunity and how you can begin building your own personal wealth by helping others.

The benefits that come from studying this toolkit are many. You'll change your current beliefs about how you can make money. *You'll enhance your ability to attract and generate your own wealth.* You'll learn more about who I am and why I'm the real deal. Not least of all, you'll learn how you can get the respect and admiration you deserve.

Best of all, it's completely free of cost and risk.

To request this free money-making toolkit just visit my web site at **www.CashFromRelationships.com/702** or call my 24 hour toll-free automated request line at **1-800-936-0121 ext. 702** and my staff will rush your package out right away.

Why not do it now while you're thinking of it? Your new adventure in life is about to begin!

FIGURE 11.1 **Sample Advertorial.** An advertorial is an ad in a magazine that is designed to look more like content than an ad. It generally tries to match the editorial style of the media in which it runs. This example shows how an advertorial might look. Big headlines at the top and shaded or coupon style offer boxes at the end of the copy are powerful elements of this type of ad.

Elements of a Successful Gravitational Marketing Print Ad

Let's talk more about how to format your print ad. Make sure that your print ad includes a headline. A headline should be one big bold statement that promises a big benefit, a big solution, and that makes the reader want to read the rest of the ad. The headline should be an ad for your ad. Don't use the headline to sell the product or the next step.

That's the mistake that far too many people make. All you're really trying to do here is sell them on continuing to read. In many cases, you may include a subheadline too. Though smaller than your headline, it will expand on the statement you made in your headline and make them to want to read even more.

How to Write a Good Headline

For an effective headline, you want to make sure that it falls into one of three categories or combines elements from these three categories:

1. *News-style headline:* This type of headline emulates what you would see in a newspaper that features, announces, or warns about something newsworthy. An example of this type of headline is: "Florida Woman Invents New Cream That Eliminates Wrinkles."

2. *Self-interest headline:* We've found this to be the best type of headline. This headline type appeals to people at the most sacred levels of their inner desires. It should be benefit driven and focus on benefits derived from Maslow's hierarchy of needs. For example: "Remove Your Wrinkles and Look 20 Years Younger in 15 Days or Less—Guaranteed!"

3. *Curiosity headline:* Says something to peak someone's curiosity so that they want to read more. This type of headline is generally *not* effective if used exclusively without combining one of the other types. This headline type is overused and often lacks the meat needed to get the reader's attention. It is best used in conjunction with a news or self-interest type headline. When combined with self-interest, it can be enormously powerful: "Could This Wrinkle-Removing Cream Have Been Used by Ancient Greeks?"

You can combine more than one type of headline to make an even more powerful headline using a headline and subheadline combination. Combining a curiosity headline with a news-style headline or a self-interest headline with a news-style or curiosity headline will help you create a more powerful headline.

Keep in mind that the purpose of the headline is simply to draw the reader down to the body of the ad. Then, each paragraph of that ad should bring them to the next paragraph, creating a downhill slope through your copy to your offer at the end of the advertisement, which gets them to take the next step.

Bonus Resource

Jim and Travis' Powerful Headline Examples

Headlines are an essential element of any marketing you may do. But why reinvent the wheel? There are so many great headline formulas that have been written and tested by marketing masters over the years.

This resource will give you examples of headlines and formulas you can use to craft powerful headlines in a fraction of the time. This is a special gift from us and you can get it at www.GravityBook.com/bonus.

Using Subheadlines in Your Copy

You might want to look at writing miniheadlines for paragraphs throughout your ad, if the publication you're working with uses subheadlines. You wouldn't have to create them for each paragraph, but you would certainly want to hit hot buttons and move the reader along to the next section every few paragraphs. These miniheadlines can be very powerful because people tend to be lazy and only read those, which will help move those people to the end of your ad so that they can take the next step.

Subheadlines also reduce eyestrain and fatigue while reading a long block of copy, which is what advertorial-style ads generally contain. They also keep your readers interested and make the ad look easier to read. Appearing to be easy to read is very important when you have a lot of sales copy. Keep in mind that the more you tell, the more you sell, so these ads can be very long.

From the Trenches

When is the last time you picked up and read a newspaper? Can you remember it?

For some of us, it wasn't that long ago. Can you remember anything about the paper the last time you looked at it?

If you can't remember anything, take a quick look at a newspaper right now . . .

What is the first thing you notice?

The first thing you notice is the headline.

Headlines are the most important element in the newspaper. Why? Because even though the paper contains a great deal of content, those headlines grab the reader's attention and draw them into the meat of the articles.

Can you imagine what a newspaper would be like if it didn't have any headlines?

It would be almost unreadable.

So many businesses make the mistake of not using headlines when they engage in advertising.

Some businesses get really creative and use the company name for the headline of their ad. This is really prevalent in the yellow pages.

Your business name is not a headline. Who really cares about your company name? Other than you, that is.

The absence of headlines and using your name as the headline of an ad are two *huge* and costly advertising mistakes that businesses make, but they both can be easily avoided.

Think of a headline as an advertisement for your advertisement. Your headline should get the reader's attention so he or she reads the next line of copy in your ad.

Every ad you run needs to have a powerful headline that engages your prospect, creates curiosity, and delivers an overwhelming benefit to the reader for continuing to read your ad. Your gravitational positioning statement (GPS) is a great thing to use as a headline of your advertisement.

Writing the Body Copy

When you write copy for your ad or marketing piece, we recommend one very specific copywriting formula—the problem-agitate-solve formula. That means you begin your copy by discussing the problem that your product or service solves for the reader.

You should exploit the pain and discomfort that your readers have, their fears, the bad things that are happening to them, or the bad things that will happen to them. If you can't think of the problem, circumstance, or issue that your product solves, you may need to rethink your product or market or become better acquainted with your target.

Next, you agitate that problem. That is, rub it in. Rub salt in the wound. Whatever that problem is, amplify it. Give specific examples. Make your readers really feel bad about it. Don't feel bad about this yourself because you're also making them feel that you understand their situation and have the solution.

You should also empathize with them. A very important part of this formula is to blame somebody or something, not the reader for the problem. You want the reader to feel like he's on your side of the table; that you are together and he's nodding his head agreeing about how bad the problem is or how awful the cause of that problem is. Essentially, you try to come around to the other side of the table, put your arm around the reader and say, "It's us against them. We have a problem and we are going to solve it together."

Now you swoop in like the knight on the white horse with the solution, and you talk about the solution, what can be done, how things can be better, and ultimately, you tell him that the solution can be found by taking the next step, which is requesting your free information.

You want to make it seem as though the free information you're offering is a silver bullet, and with one shot it is going to take care of the problem, and everything will be fine. Of course, your free widget will deliver some valuable information to help solve the problem, but ultimately, they're going to need to go further into a relationship with you to eliminate the problem and pain that they're encountering.

Now that you have a good idea how you're going to create your ad, let's talk about where you should place the ad.

$ **Expert Resource**

T.J. Rohleder and his wife Eileen started their marketing company in a small Kansas town in 1988 with only a few hundred dollars they got from selling a beat-up 1985 Chevy van. With loads of studying and help from experts, they turned that few hundred bucks into over $10 million within five years.

Now T.J. and Eileen help people who want to get into business for themselves with many different business opportunities. What T.J. knows about copywriting and print advertising can fill many books. It's through the use of effective copywriting and advertising that T.J. has built his empire.

To get more information about effective copywriting and print advertising go to the Gravitational Marketing resource site at www.GravityBook.com/print.

Techniques 13 and 14: Daily and Weekly Local Newspapers

You're familiar with these—major, daily newspaper publications in your city. You may have one or two depending on the size of your area.

You also have the neighborhood publications, which are the second level publications that cover a small area of town. These are often small, weekly publications.

Here in Orlando we have the *Orlando Sentinel* as the large, city publication and on our side of town, which is the east side of Orlando, we have the *East Orlando Sun*—a smaller, second-tier weekly publication. It's delivered to our driveway each week and talks only about very localized information. Both of these types of publications have lots of advertisers in them. You can be in one or both publications depending on your particular market.

If you're trying to reach people in a very specific geographic area, say a five-mile radius or just in a certain part of town, then it may not make sense to spend the money to be in the large, daily, city newspaper. Especially when you're just getting started, the smaller, local newspaper may make more sense for you.

But if the people you're trying to reach are all over your city, and you're looking for a far greater number of leads, then you may find that the daily, city newspaper makes more sense. Of course, you'll also find that the daily paper is far more expensive than the weekly paper.

Technique 15: Local Business Papers

If you're trying to reach a business audience in your city, the newspapers we just discussed may not be the best place for you to advertise. Your small neighborhood paper and your large city paper are going to reach a broad general audience, mostly made up of consumers. Of course, those consumers will be workers. They'll be business owners. Their careers will run the gamete of professions. But if what you're offering is only geared toward the business crowd, you would be better off advertising in a business journal magazine. Most cities and towns have a magazine like this for the business crowd.

Technique 16: Local Magazines

Local magazines offer good opportunities for advertisers. These publications may cover the whole city, the whole region, or they may cover certain parts of the city or even certain subcultures. Depending on your geography, you may find that a certain magazine will suit your offer and message better. Magazines tend to be monthly rather than daily or weekly.

You can look at these magazines to determine whether they reach a high-end, middle-class, younger, or an older audience. Magazines tend to be very specific in who they reach as they are typically written for a certain group of people and nobody else. These are called subcultures.

Gays and lesbians probably make up one subculture group in your local area. Senior citizens are another subculture group. There are magazines published for gays and lesbians, seniors, $100,000 and up lifestyles, college students, and even magazines published for parents.

In every city, there are multiple publications for many different audiences. These magazines may also resemble tabloids or newspapers. If your product or service is perfect for someone in one of these sub-culture groups, one of these magazines may be the perfect marketing opportunity for you.

Technique 17: Industry Trade Publications

If you're trying to reach people of a certain profession, then you more than likely want to reach them on a national scale because the numbers will typically be very low locally. To reach those people on a national scale, you should take a look at trade publications.

Every profession and industry has magazines or journals written for that industry. A quick Internet search will usually reveal some of them. If, for instance, you are trying to reach plumbers, you need to advertise in a national magazine for plumbers. Magazines are available for almost any profession you can name—dentists, chiropractors, nurses, and even speech-language pathologists.

If you have a national product or service business, you can utilize these trade publications in a very interesting way. Let's say you have a product or your entire line of products works well for people in a specific industry, but it's not necessarily specific to that industry. It's for a lot of people and can be utilized across industries, but you know you have tons of customers who happen to be plumbers, auto mechanics, or IT professionals.

You can write an ad specific to those professions and place it in their trade publications. You can show the people in those professions how to use your product in a way that's specific for them. You can open up a whole new market and marketing opportunity for your business that may not have occurred to you.

While your competitors are advertising on a broad, national scale, you could choose the niche trade publications. With this strategy, you can advertise your products and services in a place with a lot less competition for the type of product you offer, which makes it far easier to position yourself as an expert.

Consider an attorney who works nationally, but who decides to cater to event planners. This attorney can position herself as an expert in this industry and will likely have very little competition. She is a big fish in a small pond instead of a small fish in a big pond. Ideally, you should be a big fish in many small ponds.

In addition to trade publications, many different employment or business types have trade associations. Going to the association's publication can be beneficial and can also give you instant creditability. Most of those associations are always looking for additional advertisers and content.

Technique 18: National Hobby Magazines

National hobby magazines are also great publications for advertising. Whether you're trying to reach golf, motorcycle, tattoo, guitar, cooking enthusiasts, or stamp collectors; there is a publication out there nationally for every hobby or subculture group you could dream of.

The easiest way to find out what's available for your target prospects is to go to your biggest local bookstore and peruse the magazine section. You will see hundreds of different magazines. Pull them off of the shelf and flip through them to examine different advertising opportunities. Study the kinds of topics they discuss, and picture how you can fit your product or service into them.

Technique 19: Classified Ads in National Newspapers and Business Magazines

We're talking about national general interest publications such as *USA Today* and *Business Week*. You'll find that these publications are the most expensive options. In many cases, a full-page ad can cost more than $100,000. The audience that you reach is very broad with a high volume. These magazines and newspapers have circulations of hundreds of thousands to millions of readers. You may find that your lead generation count will be in the hundreds and thousands with a single ad in these publications. Even though these are very expensive, there are economical ways to advertise in them.

You could run a small classified ad in the back of the publication. If you have a limited budget, but you know that advertising in this magazine would be perfect to reach the people that you want to sell to, this is a less expensive way to go. You can generate many leads with a classified ad by printing a headline, similar to what you would do for a larger ad, along with a web site address or phone number to learn more about the headline.

For example, a headline like "New Breakthrough Cream Eliminates Wrinkles," that offers a web site or phone number where people who are interested and curious about the headline can learn more about how it works, might get people to read the rest of a longer ad.

Here is another effective way to use a classified ad. If you're selling a specific item such as homes, automobiles, or other items that are typically listed in the classified section, you could simply list your items in the classified ad and direct people to a web site or phone number to get more information on that item.

Classifieds are a cheap way to test a publication. You can take the biggest benefit you offer through your product or service, put that in the headline, and send the people to a web site or phone number for additional information. This is a cost effective way to find out what kind of response you can get. If the response is decent from the classified ad, then you know that if you spring for a larger ad in that same publication, assuming your ad copy is good, you can expect a decent response.

We always encourage you to test on a small level before you dump tons of money into an advertisement for a publication that you are unsure about. You want to test and then move up as you get good results.

Technique 20: Display Ads in National Newspapers and Business Magazines

Let's talk for a minute about how publications sell space. Typically, they're selling space from a fraction of a page up to a full page. Often you'll see them selling it by what they call column inch. This means that if the publication has three columns per page, you could buy an ad that is one column wide by one, two, three, or four inches high or two columns wide by two, four, six, or eight inches high. The number of columns wide by the number of inches tall is how you would determine the size (and the price) of the ad.

Our ultimate goal in most publications is to place a full-page ad. You want to work up to this as you test and measure because it is going to be noticed more often by more people. When we run a full-page ad, we always insist that it be placed on a right-hand page. As you flip through a publication, your eyes are almost always directed to the right side. The left side is usually in your left hand, which is pulling the pages away.

You should move from the classified ad to a smaller display ad, like one-eighth of a page. A display ad is considered nonclassified but it is still small. You should have a headline, and this time you have the space to add a little bit of copy that supports the statement in the headline. And again, you should include the offer for the free widget and how to get more information and the free item. Every form of print media uses the exact same format.

As the ad gets bigger, you can add more information about the free widget, do a better job of identifying and agitating the problem, and highlight how great the solution is. Your marketing story or your sales pitch expands to the space allotted.

When you are ready to run a half-page ad, you're going to have the opportunity to buy it in two different ways. You could buy it horizontally. With this option, you take up the top half or the bottom half of a page.

In many cases, you can buy a vertical half page, which is a column down one side of the page. When we're given the opportunity to buy a half-page ad and have to choose between vertical and horizontal, we always choose the vertical ad. It holds more copy because of the different layout possibilities. We also find that a vertical half-page ad reads easier.

As you graduate up to at least a half-page ad, you can begin to make your ad look more like an article, an advertorial. You should try to get away from the look of an ad and begin to polish your ad so that it looks more like an article in the publication.

Jim and Travis Recommend

Some print publications offer remnant space—that is, ad space that has gone unsold—at a tremendous discount. We have some powerful contacts who can negotiate this remnant space for you. Visit www.JimandTravisRecommend.com for more information.

Technique 21: Yellow Pages

Advertising in the yellow pages isn't for everyone, but many people who *could* benefit from yellow pages advertisements are not.

We're going to share a little insider information on some of the categories in the yellow pages that get searched more than any others. If you are in one of these categories, then you definitely need to spend your marketing dollars here. If you are not listed here, that doesn't necessarily mean you shouldn't. You just need to analyze things a little more to discover if your prospects may be looking for you in the yellow pages. Here are a few of the top yellow pages' listings:

- Auto dealer, new or used.
- Auto parts or auto repair industry.
- Beauty salons or beauty-related fields.
- Doctors, physicians, surgeons, dentists, or health-related fields.
- Hospitals.
- Lawn care.
- Lawyers.
- Pest control.
- Plumbing.
- Restaurants.

People are always looking for businesses in all of these categories.

Some people say that the Internet is making the yellow pages obsolete. But there are still many people who don't use the Internet. There are some people who are still using dial-up and can't use the Internet effectively. Some people just don't have computers.

We are avid Internet users, but we must say that the Internet is still not a good place to go for yellow pages listings. It just doesn't work right. You don't get the results you're looking for all the time.

There are also people at work who can't get on the Internet because they are blocked out. They have to use the yellow pages when they need something. The yellow pages get delivered right to everyone's doorstep so it's right at everyone's fingertips.

If you have something that people wouldn't think of by themselves, you certainly shouldn't bother listing your business here, but if people are actively seeking your product or service, then the yellow pages is a good place to be.

How to Make an Effective Yellow Pages Ad

Let's talk about some strategies to use in the yellow pages. The first big thing that you can do to make a yellow pages ad effective is to refuse to let the yellow pages ad representative design it for you. You're in the section with all of your competitors right around you. You need to stand out. You can't stand out when your ad was created by the same person and from the same template as your competitors' ads.

The yellow pages are pretty much the most competitive marketplace for your product simply because you are lumped into a category with all of your competitors. No other advertising media is as fierce. You're mixed up with a bunch of other people who may be selling similar products. Everybody is selling the exact same thing. If the yellow pages staff designs all the ads, then they all look the same. The designers literally use the same clip art, offers, graphics, and headlines for everyone. It's terrible.

Here's some insider, backstage information: The people who design your ad at the yellow pages are not allowed to spend any more time, energy, effort, or use anything special on one ad over another. Basically, their hands are tied. It's utterly impossible for them to make your ad any better than anyone else's.

The second biggest yellow pages mistake is using your company name as a headline. Open your yellow pages right now and look at it. You'll see 98 percent of the ads have the company name as the headline. A headline is not your company name. Your company name is almost not important, especially not at the top of the ad, especially not big and especially not bold.

You need to give them the *what's in it for me* at the top of that ad. You cannot lead with your company name. It fails the ultimate copywriting test, which is the *who cares* test. Your company name ... who cares? Nobody. It's not important. It's not a good leader. People don't care.

What you really want to accomplish in the yellow pages ad is to stop the shopping process. People are shopping. They're flipping through the yellow pages, actively making calls one after another looking for a low price, which is not what you want to offer. They're doing this because there's no buying preference in the phone book.

The main thing that you want to do is interrupt that shopping process. There are two specific ways to do this:

1. *Set up a consumer hotline with a recorded message.* In the ad, you offer a consumer hotline that educates consumers about what they need to be aware of in your industry. This could include common

scams to avoid, what they should look for, or questions they should ask when hiring someone. You position yourself as a consumer advocate instead of a salesperson. You become a trusted advisor instead of a product pusher. When this happens, you're able to deliver a long sales message disguised as consumer information. It should contain valuable information for the prospect who is looking to buy what you have to offer. It should allow them to understand the benefits and accolades of your company and how you solve these problems and prevent the scams that normally go on.

You can fit so much more into this message than you ever could in the yellow pages ad. This is vitally important for a business that can't spend large amounts of money on a yellow pages presence because yellow pages are expensive.

If you're only able to buy the postage stamp size ad in the yellow pages, you better do something that's going to get attention. If you put the name of your company and your phone number, nobody is going to call unless they are only looking for the lowest price.

But if you write, "Warning—Don't go to any nail salon until you hear these health safety tips for nail salon customers," they're going to call. A good majority of people will call to hear that and then you say, "These are the salons that have had the top health problems, this is what to avoid and how you know a salon is clean. By the way, we're offering a free manicure special at our salon and we have an A+ rating so come on down today."

2. *Deliver a buying preference.* A buying preference is a reason to choose you over your competition, and a yellow pages ad is the perfect place for it. This tells readers what you do so much better than any of your competitors. Exploit it. Put it front and center along with why it matters in the ad so as people are flipping through all the *me-too* junk, they see one ad that resonates so they say, "That's a clear choice. I'm going to pick them." They're going pick you over your competition every time for this one specific reason.

It's the GPS that we've been talking about. It's the headline of your yellow pages ad, and it stops them dead in their tracks and makes them think, "Nobody else compares." This works for all advertising and it's especially important in the yellow pages.

$	**Expert Resource**

Larry Conn asks, "Do you make these mistakes in your yellow pages ad?" Which mistakes is Larry referring to? We'll let him tell you. But before we do, you'll want to know that most likely you're making them, and it's costing you tons of money.

Don't feel bad. Most business owners who advertise in the yellow pages are making the same mistakes, and if you correct those mistakes there are massive profits to be had.

You can get more ultrapowerful and profitable information about yellow pages advertising by going to the Gravitational Marketing resource site at www.GravityBook.com/yellowpages.

How to Buy Print Media

There is a very simple method for buying print media. Rule number one is: Never buy right off of the rate card. Consider the rate card a work of fiction. It lists the most you'll ever pay. Think of it as the opening bid that you'll work down from. Understand that any time you're buying print, the rates are 100 percent negotiable.

Advertising space in general is always negotiable. It's all based on supply and demand. If they're sold out of inventory or close to it, you're going to have a hard time negotiating rates. But if they have space, which they generally do in print media, then you're going to have the opportunity to negotiate your pants off. How well you negotiate determines the rate that you pay. So you want to negotiate aggressively.

Here's a very simple negotiating tactic that we use very frequently. You'll find that print will always offer a discount as you commit to a longer term or contract. If it's a monthly publication, they'll offer a one-time rate, a three-time rate, a six-time rate, and a twelve-time rate. The rate is based on the number of times you're going to run your ad. If it's a weekly paper they offer a one-time rate, a four-time rate, an eight-time rate, all the way up to a fifty-two-time rate.

What we like to do is go in and explain that we are direct response advertisers. We say, "We carefully track every lead and know the exact cost and the exact source from which we receive each lead. There is a cost per lead that we need to achieve for this ad to be profitable for us. If running our ad in your publication is profitable, we will run the ad on a long-term basis. So what I would like for you to do is extend to us your long-term lowest rate for a one-time test run so that I can validate that your publication will work for my product or service."

This works 19 times out of 20.

After that you say, "Based on the other publications I advertise in and all the marketing tests I've done to this point, I feel confident that running my ad in your publication will be successful. When I determine that it is successful, I will continue as a long-term advertiser with your publication."

What they want to do is get you to sign a long-term contract. This lets them believe that you might sign. This doesn't mean that you're signing any paperwork though. In actuality, you just end up going month to month. As long as your checks are good, they'll keep on running your ad.

Rule number two of buying print is: The rate you pay the first month is the highest rate you should ever pay. When you go back to book month two, in most cases, they're not going to try to raise the rate on you because they want the business.

In fact, you can always renegotiate. Even if your first rate was at a discount, you can still say, "Well I'm going to run every month from now on so I want a discount for doing that." Getting a discount for running multiple months is something you flip back on them.

You never want to tell a print publication or any media outlet for that matter that it was a home run or a grand success. You'd never admit that you're raking in gold and thrilled with the results. You always say, "It was just okay."

If you tell them that it's great, the only thing they'll do is raise your rates. You want them to always feel like they're one month or one ad away from getting cancelled. If you're running your ad in more than one publication, you want to let each one know that they're in competition for your advertising dollar.

Keep this in mind, too. In many cases, there are other benefits and little perks they can toss you along the way if they feel they might lose you. For example, maybe they will upsize your ad if it's a matter of keeping you versus somebody else getting your money.

This all may sound ruthless, and it is. But in terms of keeping your cost per lead in line, it's a necessity for you to become a winner in media negotiation.

Attraction through Free Publicity

U sing the media to garner free publicity is an excellent and low cost way to generate leads. There are a few primary ways to generate leads using publicity and we break them down as:

- The media writes or airs a story about you.
- The media quotes you in a story they've written on a topic that your business or product is related to.
- The media features an article you have written.

You can accomplish these through a couple of different methods. First, there are two tools that you'll need. One is a press release. The second is a story of your own.

Technique 22: The Press Release

A press release is an introduction to a media outlet telling them that you have an angle. A press release lets the media know that you have something newsworthy to talk about.

Remember, the media is always looking for the next story. Newspapers need to write stories and articles. Television and radio stations need stories to create the news; magazines need stories to write articles. The media is constantly searching for newsworthy topics to discuss, which their readers will find interesting and valuable. They are also looking for experts to quote in the articles that they're writing. Journalists are experts at writing; they're not necessarily experts in the topics they're writing about. That's why they need you.

You can let the media know about you and what you have to offer by turning what you offer into a newsworthy topic or tying what you offer into a preexisting newsworthy topic. One thing that you don't want to do is write a press release that's all about you and your business but isn't newsworthy or relevant. A press release is not an advertisement. A press release is basically a tease to the media showing that you offer a solution or something of interest to their readers, listeners, or viewers.

Here's a perfect example. It's an excerpt from Joel Bauer's press release for his last book:

Author Joel Bauer to Candidates Bush and Kerry

READ MY BOOK OR LOSE THE ELECTION!

HOW TO PERSUADE PEOPLE WHO DON'T WANT TO BE PERSUADED, in stores now!

Los Angeles, CA—June 23, 2004—Using techniques from his new book: *How to Persuade People Who Don't Want to Be Persuaded* (New York: John Wiley & Sons, Inc., $24.95) Joel Bauer puts a spin on the upcoming election that even the spin doctors haven't heard!

Best of all, these are techniques that everyone can use in their daily lives—to get what they want, when they want it!

History's greatest figures have always been those who can take a story, a concept, or an emotion and connect with their audience on a truly human level. These are the maestros who can move an audience as if conducting the world's finest orchestra. These are the communicators who can transcend any setting, transform any moment, and translate any message with an almost mystical finesse.

Ronald Reagan was one such individual. Bill Clinton was another.

Now author Joel Bauer is offering his personal advice—techniques not only for candidates Bush and Kerry to sway the undecided or convert those who *have* decided—but also for all those dealing with life challenges.

$ **Expert Resource**

Dave Lakhani is one of those people who fascinates you from the moment you meet him. He is a former cult member turned marketing guru and a personal friend. Dave is a highly acclaimed speaker and author of *Persuasion—The Art of Getting What You Want* and *Power of an Hour*. Big and bold describes Dave's look, attitude, and results. Dave does many things to help business owners take their businesses to the next level. One major technique that Dave recommends is the use of publicity. The press can be a highly valuable tool for expert positioning and lead attraction.

For more information about leveraging the press, visit the Gravitational Marketing resource site at www.GravityBook.com /press.

Joel's press release was very successful, and it resulted in many media appearances for him. He appeared on several television shows and was written up in several print publications. The reason it was so effective was because it tied in to what was already going on, what was already being discussed in the news at that time. During the presidential election year, many people were discussing the candidates and who was going to win. Then along came this author's press release and his book and his challenge to the candidates: "Whoever reads my book is going to win the election."

That was a different angle on an existing media topic. That's what news outlets are looking for. They're looking for a new angle. They had to talk about the presidential race every single day in their print publication, on their television station or radio station. They were going to do that because that's what was hot, but they needed a new spin on it.

If you can offer a new spin on an already hot media topic, you're going to have a much easier time getting in. It goes back to the adage that was created by the copywriter Robert Collier who said, "You've got to enter into the conversation that's already going on inside the minds of the customers."

In this case, the media professional is the customer because you're trying to get them to pay attention. You need to determine what's on their mind right now. In Joel's case, it was the election. Joel was able to slide in with this different spin on the election discussion. Because of that, he was able to garner a tremendous amount of free publicity.

Here are a few ideas you might want to tie in with:

- Movies, TV premiers and finales.
- Musical artists.
- Fashion icons.
- Celebrities in the news.
- Current events.
- Political topics.

Watch the shows that you would want to appear on. Find out what kind of stories they broadcast. Read the magazines and newspapers that you want to publish in. Find out what kind of stories they write. Then figure out how your product or service can tie into those types of stories.

First, you should create a big headline for your press release that says why they would want to interview or follow up with you on this particular story. The rest of the press release should talk about who you are and how you can help their readers, viewers, or listeners. You should also share your credentials and tell more about why they would want to share this story with their audience.

Tease them with the press release so they will call you for the interview. You want to get them on the phone before you tell the full story. You can't tell the full story in a press release anyway because the press release shouldn't be longer than one page. There, you only have a short space to make your case.

Use that small space to tie into what the viewers are already interested in and what's already going on that's newsworthy. Create a different spin, a different angle on that, and use the press release to tease them. Mention why the story is hot and different and why you have the credentials to talk about the topic. Tease them to take the next step—to call you for an interview. You should use your press release just like your hook and permit in your ads.

Use your interview as an opportunity to make your free offer. This is how you can leverage a public appearance into a lead attraction technique.

From the Trenches

We often mention the concept of entering the conversation already taking place in your customers' minds. The basic idea is to talk about what your customers are talking about. Waltz right into their minds, break into their conversation, and get on the same wavelength as them.

Why not combine this idea with the powerful mouthpiece of the press?

Here's what I'm talking about. Watch the news closely and pay attention to pop culture. Find out what's on everybody's mind. Then take one of those concepts, and find a way to tie it into your business.

Copywriter Craig Garber did this with the death of Richard Pryor. He wrote a press release that explained what Richard Pryor knew about marketing that most business owners don't. Turns out, at that time, Richard Pryor was one of the fastest growing searches online. Craig shared in the action with a relevant piece of information.

You could do that, too. What current events or pop information relate to you? *American Idol* begins again each year, and you can bet millions of people will be searching and reading about it.

So what do you do with these press releases? For one, submit them to an online press release distribution site. You could also submit the release to a wire service or you could simply send it to your local newspaper.

Here's one last tip, act fast. These stories usually don't last long.

Technique 23: Expert Articles

Another thing that you can do is write an article for a publication. This works really well for local media and trade magazines. You can write articles as an expert in your area of expertise and submit those to your local media. Mostly, this is for print publications. As we said before, you want to read the publications you're trying to get into. You could call them and build a relationship with the editor.

Let's say you're a car dealer and there's a weekly newspaper in your area. You could tell the editor, "I write articles on the transportation needs of our community, and I would love to submit a series of articles for the newspaper."

Many of our clients have become featured columnists in their local newspapers. They've done it by submitting articles on a regular basis under their topic of expertise, which ties into the community and shows the benefits of their product or service to potential customers. At the end of these articles, there's always a soft offer for additional information and the free widget, which again is a lead generation mechanism.

$ | **Expert Resource**

Steve Harrison wants to get you booked on national television and radio. Steve has *hush-hush* insider contacts and booking secrets that are virtually unknown except to top $5,000-per-month publicists. Needless to say, he's the certified expert on attracting leads through publicity appearances on radio and TV.

Radio and TV publicity can bring in droves of leads. Who gets on radio and TV? Experts of course. Another reason why you need to become one.

We've used many of Steve's techniques and programs to create powerful publicity strategies that get media people to sit up and take notice of us and many of our clients.

(continued)

Steve's company helped launch such bestselling books as *Rich Dad Poor Dad* and *Chicken Soup for the Soul*. He shows entrepreneurs, self-promoters, and authors how to attract millions of dollars worth of free publicity.

For more information on harnessing the pulling power of radio and television publicity, visit the Gravitational Marketing resource site at www.GravityBook.com/rtv.

Attraction through the Internet

The Internet offers businesses of all shapes and sizes a wide variety of very powerful ways to generate leads, but the biggest thing to keep in mind when thinking about using the Internet is that it is not free.

Many people falsely believe that the Internet is the place to be because it costs nothing. That statement is false. That belief is dangerous. The Internet costs something; it either costs time or actual dollars and cents. Typically, you'll find that the more money you spend, the greater results you'll receive with more control over the results.

It is true that you can generate leads off the Internet without spending a single dollar. That is an option. But typically to do that you have to invest at least some time. And if you're a business owner, your time has value.

Many people may wonder, "Why are you discussing the Internet in a book about lead generation and attracting business? Isn't the Internet a business all on its own?" The answer to that question is no.

The Internet is simply a media outlet just like radio, television, newspaper, and all of the other media opportunities we have discussed throughout this book. The Internet is a tool that the business owner can use to generate leads. There are multiple lead generation opportunities available online at various price ranges using various methods. And the different opportunities deliver different levels of effectiveness. We're going to talk about the major opportunities right here.

Technique 24: Pay per Click

One of the biggest opportunities on the Internet for generating leads, and the one that we use most frequently, is pay-per-click advertising.

Pay-per-click advertising is a medium made available to us by search engines such as Google, Yahoo, and MSN. Those are the major search engines and constitute the vast majority of all searches done on the Internet. They have created systems that allow advertisers to bid on the maximum amount they are willing to pay for a click when someone searches particular keywords they have chosen.

When you agree on a price per click, the search engine begins to show your ad when someone searches a keyword that you have bid on. When the person sees your ad, if they are interested in it, they may click on it. When they click, they will be redirected to your web site. This is what you pay for.

For instance, somebody does a search for a plumber in Baltimore and a list of directories and plumbers comes up in the search engine (Figure 13.1). On Google, you will see a list of results on the right-hand side under the sponsored links section. These are ads that are shown at no cost to the advertiser. When somebody clicks on their ads, advertisers will pay up to their maximum bid price for the person to be redirected to their web site.

Pay per click allows you to be at the top of the search engine immediately, the same day you start. Pay per click allows you to target web searchers by the particular keyword that they are searching so that your ad only appears when someone searches something that's relevant to what you offer. It allows you to select people by geographic areas. If you only want to reach people in your state, town, neighborhood, country, or in some other country or any specific geographic area in the world, even a zip code or a radius around your place of business, that is possible.

Pay per click allows you to determine what's going to be displayed in your ad. Without pay per click, your listing is shown on the left side of the search engine in what's known as the organic search results. These are unpaid results. In an organic result, the search engine typically determines what text from your web site is going to be shown. With pay per click, you have the opportunity to write your own text as an ad, which gives you the opportunity to entice somebody to actually click and visit your site.

Please note that on the Internet hook and permit ads prevail. Just like any other offline media, the goal when generating leads on the Internet should be to offer a free widget unless what you're selling is very low cost. This should be done on a web page whose sole purpose is to offer that free widget and capture the contact information of the person who's requesting the widget.

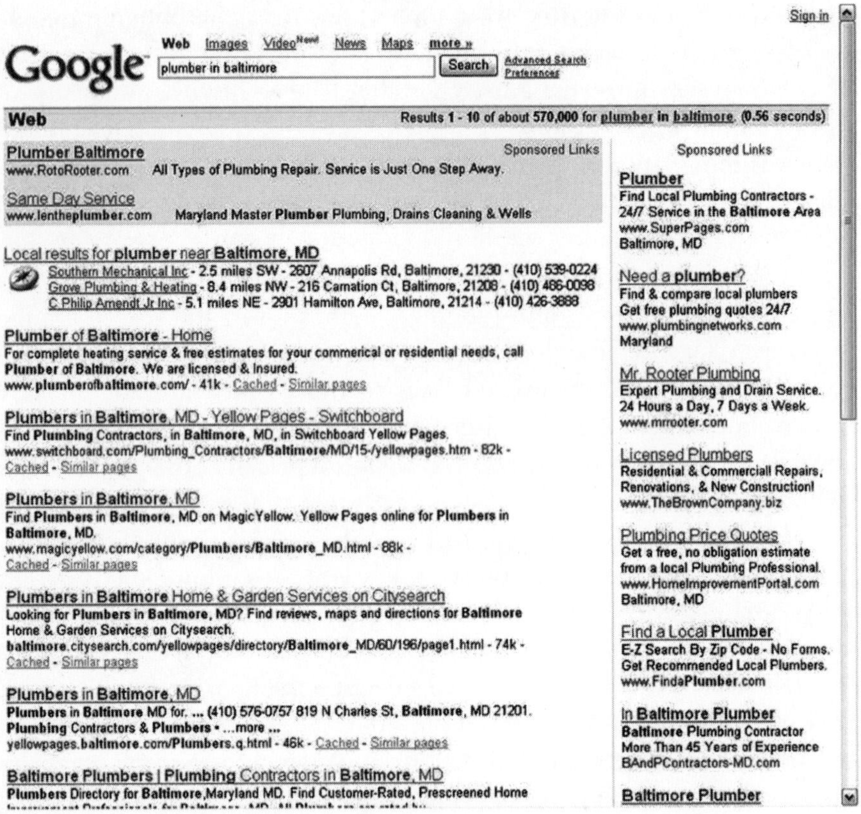

FIGURE 13.1 **Google Screen Shot.** When you use Google Adwords, your ads show in the sponsored links section of the search results. This photo shows both the organic, search engine selected results on the left and the ad-based, pay-per-click placements on the right. With Google Adwords, you can be at the top of the search engine in hours instead of months with five dollars the same day you start.

No matter which Internet marketing method you choose, the prospect should always end up in the same place—on your web page requesting your free widget. That's the intermediate goal of Internet marketing.

With pay per click, someone clicks your ad and ends up on the web page that you developed that offers your free widget. When they request your widget, they become a lead. Congratulations, you just generated a lead online.

We've found that following up with those leads offline makes the sales process work most effectively. Most companies already have an offline sales method or process. Whether it is by phone, in person, or by mail, your normal follow-up process must occur when you generate a lead from the Internet. Just because the lead came from the Internet doesn't mean that they will only want to communicate with you via e-mail and the web site. You should immediately take that lead and put it into your standard follow-up process, whatever that may be.

Expert Resources

Dave Dee is the "marketing magician" and a true expert when it comes to taking online leads and converting them to sales using offline marketing. Using offline and online marketing creates an unbeatable combination that helps you generate more profits faster and get much more consistent results. But sometimes it can be tricky.

Dave takes the mystery out of it because he's got real from-the-trenches experience. He does it himself every day and makes *"mucho deenaro"* for himself and his clients.

To get more insider information about how to use this on-line to offline strategy effectively, hop on over to the Gravitational Marketing resource site at www.GravityBook.com/offline.

From the Trenches

Recently, I was shopping for braces (a.k.a. suspenders) to go along with a few new suits. It was the first time I'd ever shopped for braces, and I quickly learned that very few stores carry them.

I did find a lovely selection of name brand braces at a high-end department store. They featured interesting motifs like ducks, music notes, wine glasses, and footballs. That's not what

(continued)

I was looking for, although I understand that these $149 braces are quite couture.

I was looking for plain white and black braces. I had been inspired by the latest James Bond movie, *Casino Royale* (Sony Pictures, 2006). In the movie, Bond is wearing a very subtle pair of white silk braces. They were understated and elegant, and I liked them.

I was having a difficult time finding them, so I turned to the Internet. What a mess! I rarely buy anything on the Internet. I find the whole ordeal frustrating. Plus, I like to touch things before I buy them. Jim, on the other hand, buys almost exclusively from the Internet.

On my Internet search, I found dozens of sloppy web sites offering braces of all shapes and sizes. What I was confused about was why there were no professional, simple, elegant web sites. Let's face it. Who is buying braces? Probably men who have low patience levels, low attention spans, who typically would not dig through a bin of clearance underwear in search of a good deal. But these web sites were set up like that. You had to dig and look at hundreds of items to begin to understand the inventory. I was unwilling to do that.

After more searches, I came across a pay-per-click ad for a certain well-known men's retailer. This retailer had paid for an ad on the front page of the search results for "men's braces." As they should.

Normally, the worst sin of pay-per-click marketing is dumping the person who clicked on the ad into your web site's home page. Think about it. I search for "men's braces," and I land on the front page of a web site. I should land on a page that is about what I was searching for—men's braces.

What happened in this instance was even worse. I landed on a page that displayed an error message. This is a prime example of advertising waste. Somebody is in charge of this pay-per-click campaign and simultaneously some other people are sitting around upstairs griping about why the marketing isn't working as it should be. I wonder why. People are finding the ad on the Internet, then clicking (which the company pays for), then landing on an error page. How could the marketing be working?

Here's how to deal with this potential monster. Act like your customers. Interact with your company in all the ways a prospect might. Call your office, call your hotline, go to your web site, complete an opt-in form, click your pay-per-click ad, and so on. Go on a frantic search for the holes in your funnel to find out where you are losing potential clients.

$ Expert Resource

Although he doesn't know it, Perry Marshall was one of the very first people to influence the way we think about marketing. Perry is the de facto expert on the topic of Google Adwords. One of our favorite things about Perry is that his content stays current and fresh, and he stays on the bleeding edge of pay-per-click marketing and other online marketing strategies. His training is perfect for the do-it-yourselfer who wants to learn to master online lead attraction. Perry's an expert at integrating personality and emotional appeal with technical information and sales.

To learn more about the power of Google Adwords and how to use it in your business, visit www.GravityBook.com/google.

Technique 25: Web Site Optimization

Web site optimization is a process that organizes the content on your web site so that it is search engine friendly. What we mean by search engine friendly is that it helps search engines recognize the site. They'll find the site. They will search the site. They will index the site in their databases. Most important, they will show the site somewhere in the search results, preferably high in the results. Optimization is about perfecting and optimizing the content that is on your web site so that it moves higher and higher up in the search results.

The idea is that you don't pay anything when someone clicks your web site when it is displayed in the organic search results—the results on the left. When done properly, you can generate leads for free.

Changes that you make on your web site to enhance your search engine friendliness are considered on-site optimization.

The other aspect of web site optimization is off-site optimization. This is when other web sites that are relevant to the topic that you're discussing place a link to your web site on their web site. This can be done in many different ways:

- People write articles about you on their web sites.
- Other web sites list your web site in a directory.
- Online articles or press releases list a link back to your web site.
- Links to your web site are mentioned on discussion forums and blogs.

Search engines want as many links as possible pointing back to your site. They want the sites that are linking to you to be relevant and valuable sites as well, not just junk sites that nobody visits.

In a best-case scenario, you should do a search on your topic and take the top 25 listings that come up and then have those web sites link to yours. This is a smart strategy because you will have links on sites that are already top picks linking to your site, which will boost the credibility and quality of your site in your prospects' minds.

There is no charge when someone clicks on your link, however, search engine optimization is not free. It's a highly specialized process that business owners should not engage in alone. In our opinion, only optimization specialists and firms should engage in this, and it will cost you money. In some cases, it could cost you more money than running pay-per-click ads.

The process of optimization isn't an exact science. It's complex and the rules change quite often, so you need somebody to continually optimize your on-site and off-site presence. Depending on whether that makes sense for you both from a lead generation standpoint and from an economical standpoint, optimization may or may not be sensible for your business.

Another point we want to make here is that just because your site is optimized, and you now rank high up in the search rankings doesn't necessarily mean you're going to generate the same number of leads that you would have using pay-per-click. The web site has to be set up to capture contact information for those leads to be valuable.

Jim and Travis Recommend

You don't want to attempt search optimization on your own. Your time is far more valuable. Instead, we recommend using certain experts to help make the job faster and easier. Visit www.JimandTravisRecommend.com for more information.

Technique 26: E-Zine

Another opportunity to generate leads online is by advertising in an e-zine. An e-zine is simply an online or e-mail newsletter. Just like printed publications, there are e-zines for every niche and subculture you can think of.

E-zines are usually created by people who have already generated a list of followers who read their information, and eventually, e-zines offer opportunities for advertising. You can buy advertising space in e-zines the same way you would in print publications. You can buy it in the form of a link in the e-zine, a listing in the e-zine, and sometimes you can buy article space in e-zines. Even banner-type advertisements are available.

The point here is targetability. You can find the prospects you're looking for because these e-zines are set up and sent to groups of people by specific topics. You can find the e-zines that correlate with the type of target you're trying to reach, and you can pay for placement in those e-zines.

Just be sure to make an offer for your free information. All the same rules that apply in print advertising apply here, too.

Technique 27: Online Articles

Another method for generating leads online is through online articles. You can simply do a search for online article sites and you will find an enormous number of them throughout the Internet.

You can write articles and post them to these free online article sites. You become featured as an expert because you're writing articles. Those articles have a tendency to spider—create a little web for you—all across the Internet. When you post to multiple article sites, people will take that content and post it on their web sites.

E-zine publishers will also take content from these article sites and publish it in their e-zines. Every time they do that, you get credit, usually in a little box at the end of an article that says who wrote it, who they are, and how you can learn more.

This is where you put your free widget offer. By doing these articles, your message gets spread. In addition, this is a very good way to position yourself as an expert throughout the Internet for free.

It's a volume game. The more articles you write and the more sites you post to, the more traffic you will get to your site. Typically one or two articles won't generate many results. You can't depend on a small effort to leverage any large results. You need to be posting multiple articles to dozens, if not hundreds, of different article sites.

This is a free method to position yourself on the Internet. Articles also help you with your optimization efforts.

Jim and Travis Recommend

There's a valuable tool that you should know about that can help you rapidly submit your article to thousands of online article sites. Visit www.JimandTravisRecommend.com for more information.

Technique 28: Blogs

Something else that helps you with optimization, placement, and quality is writing a *blog*. A blog is simply a web log or a web diary where, as an expert, you write your thoughts about a topic. You can write daily, weekly, or however often you would like. The more you update the content on your blog, the more relevant the search engines find your content to be.

Blogs are a way to keep your potential customers coming back to you again and again for more information. You create an audience of readers who read your input on a regular basis.

A blog basically gives you a chance to hold the microphone. When you're writing a blog, you create your own media whether you have 10 people, 100 people, or 1000 people who read it. It's your blog. You get to say what you want to say.

First of all it's good to provide a mix of three things on your blog:

1. One-third should be personal content.
2. One-third should be technical content.
3. One-third should be emotional content.

You should tell stories. Include personal stories about what's going on in your life and heartfelt stories that relate to the technical aspect of what you do. Also include information about the problems you solve and the issues you deal with for your customers in your business. You should give advice and tug on the heartstrings of the people who are reading.

A blog is a relationship builder. It creates a following for you. It creates a place where you can build ongoing bonds with potential customers and even with current customers. Don't forget to slip in an offer for your free widget at the end of every blog post.

To get readers to your blog, you need to use what are called *blog-listing sites*. At these sites, people can search for blogs on certain topics, which gets them a return list of related blogs. You can post your blog on these sites. By posting your blog on these different sites, people will find your blog and begin reading it.

If they find what you write interesting and relevant to their problems, they'll keep coming back and reading. That's a way you can generate leads via blogs.

Another thing that you can do with the blog is create a video blog. This is where you record yourself on video and post those videos to your blog on a regular basis instead of typing the content in a written format.

$ **Expert Resource**

To be successful in business and entrepreneurship, you have to keep up with the changes that occur in your industry and in the landscape of business, marketing, and entrepreneurship. We have found the best way to do this is to go where information is generated, ideas are spawned, and new trends incubated—blogs.

Blogs can help you keep your finger on the pulse of what's new and allow you to lead your field and be knowedgeable. Here are the top blogs we keep in our RSS aggregators and rely on to stay current and razor sharp.

ProBlogger

Darren Rowse is a full-time, blogging professional. His blog is dedicated to helping other bloggers learn the skills of blogging, share their own experiences, and promote the blogging medium. Visit his blog at www.problogger.net.

Like It Matters

Brian Oberkirch is a social media marketing consultant. *Like It Matters* is Brian's personal blog where he writes about social media, community-based marketing, and technologies that revolve around relevance. Visit his blog at www.brianoberkirch .com.

Web Ink Now

David Meerman Scott is the author of *The New Rules of Marketing & PR* and works directly with technology companies, entrepreneurs, and organizations to harness the power of the Web and new media for success. On his blog, he teaches you how to use online thought leadership and viral marketing strategies to grow your business. Visit his blog at www.webinknow.com.

Copyblogger

Brian Clark is an Internet marketing strategist, content developer, entrepreneur, and recovering attorney. *Copyblogger* delivers powerful copywriting tips for online marketing success. The site is easy to navigate and the posts are both visually stimulating and priceless. Visit his blog at www.copyblogger.com.

Go Big Network

Wil Schroter is a fellow serial entrepreneur who has started nine companies. A college dropout and wannabe actor, Wil made good and now has a serious desire to help others *Go Big*. His blog is a master's level course in entrepreneurship and his *Go Big Network* is a resource no entrepreneur should be without. Visit his blog at www.gobignetwork.com/wil/.

Micro Persuasion

Steve Rubel is a senior marketing strategist with Edelman, the largest independent global PR firm, and Steve is the go-to guy for revolutionary media and marketing. Steve is charged with helping Edelman identify, test, incubate, and champion new forms of communication. On his blog, Steve discusses and analyzes how technology is revolutionizing media and marketing in a fun-to-read, nontechnical way. Visit his blog at www.micropersuasion .com.

(continued)

Scobleizer

Robert Scoble is the coauthor of *Naked Conversations: How Blogs Are Changing the Way Businesses Talk with Customers,* an American blogger, and a technical evangelist. His hugely popular blog came to prominence when he was a technical evangelist at Microsoft. Now, it paves the way for new technology and gives a seasoned veteran's view on what's new and hot. Visit his blog at http://scobleizer.com.

Marketing Technology Blog

Doug Karr is the director of technology for Patronpath, a marketing and eCommerce company serving the retail food and restaurant industry. His blog is a tasty treat for anyone interested in marketing and technology. Doug's great personality shines through on his posts and it makes the blog a fun read. Visit his blog at www.douglaskarr.com.

Small Biz Trends

Anita Campbell is the CEO of Small Business Trends LLC, a media and information company. She is also editor of the highly popular *Small Biz Trends* blog. Anita closely follows trends in the small business market and technology, and she delivers the goods on her blog, through her newsletter, and on her *Small Business Trends* radio show. Visit her blog at www.smallbiztrends.com.

Master New Media

Robin Good is an online publisher and new media communication expert who researches, writes, and publishes information on the effective use of new technologies for learning, business, and social change. His blog is treasure trove of business building information and new media insight. Robin definitely has a zest for life and a passion for putting it out there. Visit his blog at www.masternewmedia.org.

Writing White Papers

Michael Stelzner is one of the leading authorities on the topic of writing and marketing white papers. He has written white papers for the world's most recognized companies, including Microsoft, FedEx, Motorola, Monster, Hewlett-Packard, and SAP. Michael's blog is the only one exclusively dedicated to the topic of white papers. Call them what you want—special reports, information widgets, industry bulletins—white papers should be a key component of your marketing process, and Michael provides loads of valuable information on his blog and in his book, *Writing White Papers: How to Capture Readers and Keep Them Engaged*. Visit his blog at www.writingwhitepapers.com/blog.

Your Guide to Entrepreneurs

Scott Allen is a 20-year veteran technology entrepreneur, executive, and consultant. He helps organizations build better business relationships on the Internet using online communities, social networking sites, blogs, mailing lists, discussion forums, and more. His blog is a source for entrepreneurial insight from a guy who's walked the walk. Visit his blog at http://entrepreneurs.about.com.

Guy Kawasaki

Guy Kawasaki is an evangelist, entrepreneur, investment banker, venture capitalist, and columnist for *Entrepreneur Magazine*. Previously, he was an Apple Fellow at Apple Computer, Inc. Guy is the author of eight books including *The Art of the Start, Rules for Revolutionaries, How to Drive Your Competition Crazy, Selling the Dream*, and *The Macintosh Way*. If you haven't already, check out his blog at http://blog.guykawasaki.com.

(continued)

SEO Book

Aaron Wall is an SEO guru in the real sense of the word. He is also a giver of information, time, money, and expertise. His blog is a powerhouse of SEO info. He updates it just about daily and is always on top of the new trends that make web pages rank higher and businesses grow faster. Visit his blog at www.seobook.com/node/.

PR Leads

USA Today called Dan Janal a "true Internet marketing pioneer." His views on marketing and publicity have shaped several generations of top marketers. He has consulted with IBM, American Express, and *The Readers Digest*. Because Dan is a serial entrepreneur, PR veteran, and marketer, his blog has a refreshing real-world edge you won't want to miss. He was also part of the PR team that launched AOL. Visit his blog at www.prleads.com/blog/.

My Success Gateway

Jim Peake and Bill Samson's mission is to guide and assist others to achieve success and abundance in their lives. The more people they can help, the better. Their blog provides individuals, entrepreneurs, and small businesses with an in-depth review of tools for success. Visit their blog at www.mysuccessgateway.com.

Technique 29: Podcasts

A *podcast* is like a radio show on the Internet. You can do this using your computer and a microphone, simply recording your own program. Podcasts can include interviews, guests, or it could just be you talking.

All the subscribers to your podcast should be notified as you post new episodes. They can then download it and listen to it on their computer or MP3 player.

Once again, this allows you to create a relationship with your target prospects. The idea is to constantly offer your free widget to people who are outside your funnel. Or, if they're people who are already leads, then you can make your secondary offer—your sales offer.

You can do this in a nonoffensive way. Throughout the show, you just want to drop a line that says something like, "For those of you who are new to the podcast, you'll want to download my free widget or get my free widget by going to my web site or by calling this phone number."

This is very nonobtrusive. It's a soft-sell, but you're giving those people an opportunity to get your free item. They'll be happy to get more from you, and they'll want to take you up on your offer. Even if you have people who have already gotten the offer from you before, listening to it on your podcast won't offend them.

$ **Expert Resource**

David Scott believes that the best way to reach your buyers directly is through online thought leadership strategies including blogs, Web news releases, podcasts, e-books, and viral marketing.

His book *The New Rules of Marketing & PR* is a homerun for anyone wanting to learn how to use these emerging marketing methods to change the game and explode their business.

David is a thought leader and helps others become one too. He has created thought leadership programs that have won numerous awards and are responsible for selling over $1 billion in products and services worldwide.

To learn more about David's book, blog, and how to use new media to market your business head on over to the Gravitational Marketing resource site at www.GravityBook.com/newmedia.

Technique 30: Online Forums, Chat Rooms, and Comments

Another thing you can do to generate leads on the Internet is to post comments in online forums and chat rooms.

Think about who your potential customers are. Now think about what kinds of online discussion forums they might be visiting. For instance, if you're targeting dentists, they will probably have an online discussion forum that they use to communicate with one another.

If you sell a product to home owners, there are plenty of discussion forums about home repair, home renovation, do-it-yourself, and other home-related things where you could go to offer expert advice under those topics. While you are there, you can mention your product, your widget, and how they can get more information about it.

You want to go in as an expert to these online forums and chat rooms where your prospective customers are having relevant discussions about the market you serve. When they talk about their challenges, you could provide solutions and answers and give them an opportunity to get your free widget.

You can also visit blogs written by other people about your topic. Make comments about their posts and in your comment provide a link back to your web site. As people read these comments, they'll click on your link if they are interested. Just don't be a jerk and make irrelevant comments. Your comments should sound like they're coming from an expert and add value to the discussion.

Technique 31: Video Posting Sites

Google Video, YouTube, and other video posting web sites are very popular now. You can post short snippets of video on these sites, and it is very similar to what you were doing on your video blog or podcast.

In this case, you should make sure the clips are entertaining and content driven. You could interview an expert, talk to the viewers, or do something creative and funny. Then, you take your entertaining video and post it to Google Video or YouTube. When people search those sites for new and unique videos, they will watch what you've done.

At the end of the video, you want to drive them back to your web site where they can get your free widget. You may also, if you're good with a computer, superimpose your message on top of the video: "Get my free widget at www.xyz.com." Then people who are watching the video know where to go the entire time for the free additional information.

$ Expert Resource

Ken McCarthy organized and sponsored the first conference ever held on the subject of the commercial potential of the World Wide Web, better known as—how to make money on the Internet. Each year Ken hosts the preeminent conference for online marketers, entrepreneurs, and business owners who want to better harness the power of the Internet to sell their products and services. One of Ken's most recent endeavors has been to examine the effect and power of video on the Internet.

To learn more about how to effectively leverage video on the Internet, visit www.GravityBook.com/video.

Technique 32: Personal Networking Sites

Another emerging online lead generation strategy is the use of personal networking sites. These are sites like MySpace.com.

At MySpace.com you can put a page up about yourself or your business, positioning yourself as an expert. Then you can offer your free widget and additional content and information. You can also go to other people on MySpace and request to become a member of their friend list. MySpace becomes a viral marketing tool when you become friends with multiple people. You basically create this network of people that grows exponentially. These people visit your site, and often they'll take you up on your free opportunity.

The targeting aspect of this is not extremely powerful because it's more of a broad stroke in a general community, but it is free, and it is an opportunity for you to broadcast a widespread message. It would work very well if you have a broad audience-based product with a national audience and distribution, and especially if you're targeting a younger demographic.

Blogs, online videos, podcasts, and personal networking sites all have a tendency to be very viral in nature, meaning that the people who read and listen to them are often likely to tell other people about them because they're a new and interesting form of media. This makes these opportunities potentially powerful as lead generation tools because when other people talk about your blogs, videos, or podcasts, they're handling a marketing function for you at no cost.

$ **Expert Resource**

Timothy Seward is one of those guys who can make you gobs of money but does it from the shadows. His company ROI Revolution (great name) does something most people don't even want to, or have the capacity to, think about—metrics.

He's the guy who understands all that high-tech stuff that allows you to know where your leads come from, and whether they are taking the next step you want them to take. The data Timothy can get from Google's free tools like Google Analytics is simply astounding.

ROI Revolution manages our Google Adwords accounts and our web analytics. Since they took it over, they have produced results that have frankly been amazing.

To learn more about the power of measuring the effectiveness of your online efforts, visit the Gravitational Marketing resource site at www.GravityBook.com/roi.

14

Attraction through Radio and Television

Broadcast advertising refers to radio, television, and cable. Broadcast media is very exciting and we've had tremendous success with it. Unfortunately, it's just not right for many smaller businesses.

The key to broadcast advertising is high frequency and a fairly long-term commitment. You don't want to start and make a rash decision about continuing. You want to make a decision over time, based on an ongoing commitment to stick with that media.

If you get on television or radio, you want to stay on television or radio. You don't want to broadcast for a week and then jump off. You wouldn't want to do that because there are residual long-term effects that come from advertising in broadcast that build up over time.

We need to point out that you should see results immediately with broadcast. Don't ever listen to a representative who tells you that it takes time for your message to become effective. That's not true. Over time, results which are good to begin with will become better as the frequency of your message increases. This is truly brandscending at work.

Technique 33: Radio

Radio can be a powerful tool if you're offering something with a wide appeal. Radio stations reach many thousands of people and cast a wide net. Radio provides an opportunity to target your message based on station format. Common radio formats are:

- News/Talk.
- Adult/Contemporary (A/C).
- Rap/Hip-hop.
- Country.
- Contemporary hits (CHR).
- Classic rock.

- Rock.
- Oldies.
- Jazz.

Each format has its own unique type of audience. Additionally, a station of one format could have a much different audience than another station of the same format someplace else.

Radio stations tend to have excellent demographic data on their listeners. So you can ask for information that can help you decide if their audience is right for what you offer.

Don't be fooled into thinking that just because you serve seniors that an oldies station is the perfect place for you to advertise. Your product offering still needs to have a wide appeal, and the geographic area that you serve must be large, too.

Radio reaches a listening audience 50+ miles away from the city center. When you advertise on the radio, you pay to reach all of those people. If you only work on the east side of town, you may be wasting a lot of money by advertising on the radio.

When you advertise on the radio, you want to be sure to stick to the big benefits your offering provides. Because you only have 60 seconds to say your message (never, ever buy a 30-second radio commercial, even though the representative will urge you to consider it), you don't have many words you can say in that amount of time. In fact, a 60-second commercial really boils down to around 160 to 180 words. That's not very many. So you need to clearly identify the big benefits and the next action and spend the 60 seconds talking about those things only.

When it comes time to produce your commercial, you will have a few options. Most stations will offer to produce your ad for you for free. The problem is that they produce most of the ads, and they all begin to sound the same. If you're making the investment to be on the radio in the first place, it usually makes sense to pay a production company and a professional announcer to do your commercial. If you do decide to use the station, we highly recommend that you consider featuring your own voice in the commercial because it will sound different from the standard disc jockeys who do all the other commercials, plus it can boost your level of celebrity, credibility, and expert perception.

	Jim and Travis Recommend

Over the years, we've used a number of different production companies. We've found a few that we consider the best. Visit www.JimandTravisRecommend.com for more information.

One highly effective strategy you can use if you have a smaller budget is something called *roadblocking*. Roadblocking consists of choosing a set time every day and running your commercial during that time. Because people are creatures of habit, they will usually be listening to the same station at the same time every day. This allows you to systematically grow your advertising on the station. Once you get good consistent results from a single day commercial, you can add another.

If your budget is a little more flexible, you may consider arranging a disc jockey or *jock endorsement*. This is when a popular personality on the station uses your product or service and then tells the listeners how great you are. You do pay extra for this opportunity, but if the personality has a strong enough bond with his or her listeners it can really pay off.

In this section, we're going to share something that is easily worth $50,000. Here it is, buried in the back of the book. Most people won't realize the value, but we're committed to giving you all we got, so here it is.

If you really are ready to make a serious commitment on the radio and have a decent size budget to work with, you want to schedule your commercials like this:

- Buy 2 or 3 commercials in morning drive on weekdays.
- Buy 1 or 2 commercials during lunchtime on weekdays.
- Buy 2 or 3 commercials in afternoon drive on weekdays.
- Buy 5 commercials in the evening on weekdays.
- Buy a handful of overnight commercials each night.
- Buy several commercials on each day of the weekend.

Refuse to buy commercials in *wide* day parts. An example of a wide day part is 6 AM to 10 AM Instead, we consider morning drive 7 AM to 9 AM That's a *narrow* day part. Lunch is 12 PM to 2 PM, and afternoon drive is 4 PM to 6 PM. That's it. The stations will try to widen those day parts as much as possible and what you will find is that there's nobody listening during the fringe hours, but you pay just as much for a commercial during that time as during the peak time.

From the Trenches

Everyone knows a small change in angle can equal a huge change over long distances. The same is very true in marketing.

Marketing is all about testing and measuring. If an ad, script, postcard, flyer, or sales presentation doesn't work, try something different. It's not rocket science!

The key, however, is to pay close attention to what you change so that you can understand what makes the ad work. In fact, we recommend only changing one thing at a time.

If an ad didn't work, don't start over from scratch. Try changing just the headline. Try changing the placement. Make small changes and monitor the results. Be sure to make only one change at a time and test again. You're looking for the variable that causes the change. If you change 10 things at once, you will never know which change was the one that worked. It takes patience and fortitude.

We have a real-life example for you. This happened to a former client who had hired us to manage her radio campaign.

Her company had been running radio with one particular station. The ads never worked. No one could figure out why.

That's when we came into the picture. We created an ad that was very specific and targeted. This ad focused on benefits and barely even touched on features. The features weren't what someone would want, but the benefits were very desirable to small business owners.

(continued)

The first week ran. Zero calls came in, but we were smart enough to structure the radio buy in such a way that we could tweak, test, and understand. Specifically, we only ran spots in a single day part—the morning drive. Previously, the station had been running the spots from 6 AM to 12 midnight.

In week two, we said, "Switch all the spots to midday, 11 AM to 2 PM." Why? We wanted to make one tiny change and watch the results. We didn't think the change needed to be in the ad itself.

On the first day of this second attempt, we received an e-mail. "We've gotten four calls already!" Wow, what a big change!

If we had made more than one change, we wouldn't have known what made the difference. But, we knew with certainty that the problem was the day part. We'll be sure never to run her spots in morning drive on that station ever again. That's invaluable data.

Keep in mind, this is different for every product, every station, and in every city. That's why we test everything. Nothing works exactly the same way twice.

The next thing we always do is play a game called *beat the control*. We run the ad in a different day part and see if we can beat what's currently working best. If not, we go back and change the spot a little. Ultimately, we end up with a very solid, proven strategy for use on that station.

Technique 34: Television

Before we start this discussion, we want to clarify that television and cable are two different things. Let's explain. Advertising on television in the local market is advertising with your six big networks. These are ABC, CBS, NBC, CW, FOX, and UPN. Sometimes there's also an independent channel broadcasting in your local town.

When we say television, we're talking about buying advertising spots directly from one of these major stations. Both people who have an antenna on their television and cable viewers will see these commercials.

When you buy television, you want to buy shows. Buy the shows that your prospects are most likely to be watching. If it's a one-hour show, try to buy two commercials during the show so that the viewers see your ad twice. The station will be resistant to do that but if you insist they'll frequently give in.

The biggest downfall to television is the cost of producing commercials. If you make a big enough commitment to the station, they will usually produce your commercial for free. But most advertisers end up paying for production. The problem is that producing your commercial may require on-location shooting, possible in-studio shooting, editing time, and voice-over work. Quality television production can frequently run into thousands of dollars just for a 30-second commercial that you only run for a month or two.

For this reason we have never been tremendous advocates of television advertising for smaller companies.

Television is primarily effective for companies that work in large geographic areas centered around a city with a broad market appeal.

Of course, in a 30-second commercial, you must stay cemented to the biggest benefits you offer and a very clear next action.

Technique 35: Cable

When we talk about buying cable, we mean you're going to buy ads on stations like The Discovery Channel, The Food Network, The Science Channel, The Learning Channel, and The Golf Channel. These are the stations people pay to receive and are only offered by your local cable provider.

On cable, you want to buy shows. Because people watch the same shows week after week or night after night, you want to make sure that you buy the same shows over and over. Don't allow the sales representative to spread your ads out over different networks all through the day. Instead focus your advertising on specific, highly viewed shows.

Cable is especially effective if you are on the outskirts of the city and don't want to pay for the television or radio stations that reach all the people in the center of the city. Let's face it, if you're 35 miles outside of your city, people are not going to drive to do business with you. Cable allows you to buy different *zones*, which are geographic pockets of population. This allows you to buy only those zones that fit into your effective geography.

Cable carries with it the same production challenges as television and for this reason is not high on our recommendation list for smaller companies.

Technique 36: Outdoor

Outdoor advertising (billboards) is our least recommended type of marketing. Outdoor advertising should only be supplemental to everything else you do. It's a support media that's similar to buying a banner at the ballpark. You shouldn't expect huge results. At least when you're buying the banner at the ballpark, you're donating to a good cause, not to the for-profit billboard company. When you're buying the billboard, you're donating to a big media conglomerate where your money is like a squirt in the bucket.

Here is the big key with outdoor advertising—if you have a billboard, and you're not advertising in print or direct mail, get rid of the billboard. Cancel your billboard, buy some print ads, and send some direct mail. You'll get a lot more results out of those.

If you do have a billboard right now, and you have more than eight words on it, you need to seriously reconsider your strategy. Eight words is about the maximum that people can take in while driving.

The key to those eight words is not to be cute and clever, not to be funny. It's to offer a big benefit and communicate a next action. In fact, the best copy for a billboard is "Cracker Barrel, Next Exit" or "Turn Here." That's really about all a billboard is good for.

How to Buy Broadcast Media

We want to give you a very powerful media-buying tip here. It's based on the concept of an annual commitment. When you're ready to buy radio, television, or cable, the best way to get very low rates is to tell the representative or manager you're dealing with that you're interested in making an annual commitment.

Broadcast media inventory is sold on a supply versus demand basis, and when station representatives look out a year from now or six months from now, their inventory is basically unsold. But the inventory for this week costs a lot more because it is mostly sold. When you buy a large block of advertising over a long period of time, they average the price of the inventory over the year, which brings your overall price down. When you say you're interested in making a long-term commitment, they're willing to work with you and offer lower rates.

You should know that most standard broadcast contracts have a two-week cancellation policy. We're not suggesting that anybody lie, cheat, or steal whatsoever. What we're saying, though, is that you should say that you are interested in making an annual commitment so that you can talk about reasonable rates. You say, "If anything changes or comes up, I may need to cancel." You need to know you have that ability.

You must make sure that they don't try to slip a no cancellation policy into your contract. We've seen them try to do this before. If they try to pull that on you, find another station. There are plenty of them.

You should always have the option to cancel because you don't want to run ads with a failing station for any long-term commitment. You want to make sure that your ad produces direct results.

You're going to be testing for the first three to four weeks. Once your ad produces results, even if they're modest results, even if they're break-even results, you want to continue to run for a long period of time. You want to be on the air for a long period of time because your ad's effectiveness will increase.

Many media representatives represent multiple stations and will suggest taking your budget and splitting it up over several stations. They may also suggest doing ads on the Internet radio station and hosting a booth at an upcoming event or show. They say you'll be getting a good marketing cross section. In truth, what you're doing is spraying and praying. It's like a shotgun blast where you put a little bit here and a little bit there. What you get is nothing. Instead, you want to dominate.

Here is the domination strategy we recommend. First, you want to dominate a part of the day. This means if you're going to buy radio, then you want to dominate the morning drive; or if you're buying television, then you want to dominate morning news. You could also choose to dominate midday or evening news. You begin by dominating a specific day part on a specific station.

People are creatures of habit. They generally do the same things at the same time every day. So if you dominate the same day part on the same station over and over, these same people will hear your message over and over. That is what you want. You want to cluster. You're looking for frequency. You want to have a very high frequency in a weekly period with the same people.

You don't want to start putting a spot here and a spot there, which is what the stations will want you to do. They'll want to give you a broad 24-hour rotation schedule where your commercials will run any time within a 12- or 24-hour period. They do that to get the rates down. They do that to keep their flexibility. They will put your spots wherever they have an opening. Generally, those are in-the-toilet times. It's the people with the high-powered agencies who get the good slots, and then everyone else gets what's left.

If you don't have the budget to run two very strong weeks, rather than running two light weeks, we would run one strong week. Rather than doing a poor job on two stations, we would do a good job on one station.

Always focus and concentrate your efforts and spending.

If you do have money to buy multiple stations, you want to look for parallel audiences. If your audience is people between the ages of fifty and seventy, it's often a wise move to buy another station that has the same audience so that you can increase your frequency with those people. Most likely, they're going to flip back and forth between those stations. You want to appear omnipresent to that group of people.

Epilogue

There you have it! Gravitational Marketing on a silver platter. You've learned how to escape the rat race of traditional sales and marketing, reprogram your mind to expect rapid abundance, position yourself clearly and undeniably as an expert, solidify exactly who it is you should be doing business with, identify what makes you and your company irresistible, and tap into the sensitive emotional g-forces that make your customers buy and communicate in a way that causes prospects to Gravitate to you instead of you chasing them. This information has set you on the path to creating a business and a life that is Enjoyable, Simple, and Prosperous.

You've been exposed to 36 different ways to attract new customers. Don't take this as an exhaustive list. These are just some of the most common Gravitational Attraction Techniques that we have used with our clients over the years. There are many others available like bus benches, bathroom advertisements, and blimps, and those are just the ones that start with B.

Your local area may have opportunities that aren't available anywhere else, and nontraditional lead attraction techniques, like joint venturing with other business owners who serve customers similar to yours, are almost endless.

Just know that you always want to be on a constant quest to add new and profitable attraction techniques to your mix. The more you have, the more recession-proof and successful your business will become.

Go forth friends and start. Take action now. Implement what you've learned today, and you'll be more profitable tomorrow. Use Gravitational Marketing and you'll be on your way to a more Enjoyable, Simple, and Prosperous life.

Realize the unique responsibility you've been burdened with. Now you have a blueprint for success that you can easily and quickly model. Are you going to follow the advice we've given you? Gosh, we sure hope so.

Now that we've reached the end of this book, it's time to start talking about how we can continue our journey together. You're not alone. We're excited that you've decided to hang out with us, and we hope that you're interested in taking it a bit further. This is sort of like that awkward moment in the bar after the free drink.

We, along with our outstanding team, have assembled life-transforming tools, training, and information at www.GravityBook. com. If you haven't already visited that site to claim your free bonus resources, we encourage you to do it now before you forget.

There you will learn about additional opportunities to grow and transform your business by becoming more involved with the Gravitational Marketing community.

Oh, just one more thing. As the manuscript for this book is being finalized, the beginnings of the next book are taking shape.

There's much more to Gravitational Marketing—such as, what do you do once you attract all those leads? We're working feverishly to create a step-by-step road map that you'll be able to use to Captivate, Invigorate, and Motivate your newly attracted prospects into profitable customers and ravenous fans.

Be sure to head over to www.GravityBook.com and register there to be on the announcement list for the next book in the Gravitational Marketing series.

Defy Gravity!

How to Get More Jim and Travis

It doesn't matter where you are in the world. Jim and Travis can help you attract new customers and create a business that is Enjoyable, Simple, and Prosperous.

If you would like to learn more about how Jim and Travis and their team can help you or your company prosper, visit www.GravitationalMarketing.com where you will find information about:

- *The Gravitational Marketing® Community:* Includes a free web discussion forum, free e-mail newsletter, peer-to-peer mastermind groups, and local Gravitational Marketing networking groups.
- *The Gravitational Marketing® Business Acceleration Center:* Features coaching programs, training systems, and live events for entrepreneurs and business owners.
- *The Gravitational Marketing® Newton Network Newsletter:* A monthly marketing seminar in print written by Jim and Travis and delivered to your doorstep.
- *The Gravitational Marketing® Ultimate Free Gift:* Includes a free 60-day subscription to the *Newton Network Newsletter* and more than $597 worth of free training material.

Jim and Travis: Live! Discover how you can arrange for Jim and Travis to speak at your meeting, convention, or event, or even arrange for a private consultation for your company.

Visit www.GravitationalMarketing.com today.

How to Get More Joel Bauer

Joel Bauer can teach you to persuade in a way you never imagined possible. Not in a Dale Carnegie way. Not by smiling and tossing in people's first name as you speak with them. This is about getting people to do what you want. Particularly strangers.

His last book, *How to Persuade People Who Don't Want to Be Persuaded: Get What You Want—Every Time* and the web site www.PersuasionFoundation.com can show you how to persuade by using the techniques of professional pitchmen.

If you want to bring the secrets of showmen to the boardroom and your business and learn how to use entertainment to influence, go to www.persuasionfoundation.com and receive over $579.00 in free gifts and tools, including:

- *Joel Bauer's Persuasion Video Blog:* Features practical tips for preparing yourself to influence others and to present yourself in a way that is unforgettable.
- *Joel Bauer's Persuasion Power/Customer For Life System:* A world-class training event in your home or office via private video sessions with Joel Bauer.
- *Persuasion Power Success Blueprint:* A step-by-step blueprint for achieving rapid success using Joel's Persuasion Power system.
- *Priority Access to Teleconferences:* Where you will learn directly from Joel secrets of presentation and persuasion mastery.

Visit www.PerusasionFoundation.com today.

The Ultimate Free Gift from Jim and Travis

Copy page 227 and fax to 1-800-930-7194 or go to www .GravityBook.com/free.

Get All of These Valuable Resources for Free (total value, $539)

- Two months of the *Newton Network Newsletter* delivered to your door.
- Audio CD: *The Six Thick Bricks to Building Business Big Shots*, with guest Adam Dudley, delivered to your door.
- MP3 Audio: *How to Double, Triple, or Quadruple the Effectiveness of Your Yellow Pages Ad Now*, with guest Alan Saltz, instantly downloadable.
- Pocket book: Excerpts from *The Treasury of Quotes* by Jim Rohn, containing over 140 quotes on 20 selected topics, delivered to your door.
- E-book: *Think and Grow Rich* by Napoleon Hill, instantly downloadable.
- Special report: "Jim & Travis' Headline Cheat Sheet: How to Create Powerful Headlines That Blast Your Competition to Bits," delivered to your door.
- E-book: *Scientific Advertising* by Claude Hopkins, instantly downloadable.
- Audio CD: *The Four Fearless Factors of Becoming Sensationally Uncommon*, with guest Michael York, delivered to your door.

- E-Book: *How to Write Advertisements That Grab Your Prospects by the Throat, Make Them Whip Out Their Wallets and Beg You to Take Their Money*, instantly downloadable.

There is a one-time charge of $9.00 to cover postage for all of your free gifts and the two free months of the *Newton Network Newsletter*. You have no obligation to continue receiving the newsletter at the lowest price we offer ($29.00 per month U.S. and Canada or $39.00 per month International). If you do continue receiving the newsletter, you may cancel at anytime.

Name _____

Business name _____

Address _____

City, state, zip _____

E-mail _____

Phone _____

Fax _____

Credit card number _____

Exp. date _____

Signature _____

Date _____

Copy this page and fax to 1-800-930-7194, or go to www .GravityBook.com/free.

Providing this information constitutes your permission for Jim and Travis or Scend LLC to contact you regarding related information via the contact information you provide.

Jim and Travis Recommend

We've covered a lot of territory in this book, and you probably have a lot of ideas to get started. But you may also have a pretty long list of question marks ... like, "How do I do that?"

When we first started out, we asked that same question many times. Over the years, we have amassed a virtual phone book of tools, resources, experts, and vendors. If we didn't have these people, we could not do what we do.

As a reader, you can get access to our recommended vendors, resources, and tools. Just visit www.JimandTravisRecommend.com to find a compendium of contact information for people and tools that we use personally and that we recommend to help take your business to the next level.

The recommendations on this site are for people and resources that we rely on personally and have found to be of the highest quality.

Visit www.JimandTravisRecommend.com today.

About the Authors

Jimmy Vee and Travis Miller are young entrepreneurs with a penchant for teaching and inspiring others to build businesses that are Enjoyable, Simple, and Prosperous (ESP). They are the creators of Gravitational Marketing. They help entrepreneurs and business owners in many industries achieve a lifestyle of wealth and freedom through properly leveraged marketing efforts.

Their marketing insights have been applied around the world in countries like China, Poland, Great Britain, Holland, South Africa, and Canada. Their marketing impact has been felt in every major U.S. market and has resulted in over $10 billion in sales to date—a number accentuated by the fact that Travis and Jimmy are barely over 30.

Former college roommates, Jimmy Vee and Travis Miller stumbled into advertising after flunking out of calculus. Jim earned his MA in Organizational Management from the University of Phoenix, and Travis earned his MA in Corporate Communication and Technology from Rollins College.

Travis lives in Florida with his wife, Jennifer, and daughter, Ella. Jimmy lives in Florida with his wife, Christy, and daughter, Autumn.

Joel Bauer is, according to the *Wall Street Journal Online*, "undoubtedly the chairman of the board of corporate trade-show rainmaking." Using a compelling synthesis of magic, hypnosis, sales persuasion, and revival-show fury, Joel builds crowds from trade-show passersby and converts them into willing prospects for his clients. On witnessing this miraculous, Joel-engineered conversion process, a *Wired* magazine reporter called it "an incredible feat of mass obedience that must be seen to be believed."

Twenty million people have experienced Joel's traffic-stopping presentations for organizations such as 3M, Canon, General Motors, IBM, Intel, Mitsubishi, Motorola, Panasonic, and Philips. Millions more have seen him perform on television for networks such as ABC, CBS, NBC, CNBC, CNN, and FOX.

Although Joel continues to entertain and persuade at trade shows, he now works primarily as a speaker, teaching audiences the secrets of persuasion, sales, personal productivity, and his special brand of marketing.

He lives in California with his wife, Cherie, and children Chanelle, Briana, and Sterling.

Joel is also the co-author of *How to Persuade People Who Don't Want to Be Persuaded*.

Will You Do Us a Favor?

So you've read the book, and now we're wondering if you would take a few minutes to call a special number where you can leave your comments about what you learned and how it can or has impacted you and your business.

We and other entrepreneurs want to know what you think about it! All you need to do is call **1-800-609-9006 extension 6848** and follow the recorded instructions you'll hear.

We're going to collect the positive comments we get and put them on a Gravitational Marketing Eavesdrop Line in the near future so that other people will be able to call and listen to the comments.

You'll kinda' become famous because a lot of people will hear your comments. And if you leave your email address we'll send you a bonus gift to show our appreciation.

Again, the phone number to call is **1-800-609-9006 extension 6848.**

We really appreciate your help, and we look forward to personally listening to your messages.

To Your Success,
Jimmy Vee and Travis Miller

Index